Beyond Environment

Emanuele Piccardo
Amit Wolf

6 — 9 Off-Site: Ingalill Wahlroos-Ritter

10 — 15 Introduction: Bruno Orlandoni

16 — 37 From the City to the Environment: Emanuele Piccardo

38 — 49 The Education of an Un-Architect: Amit Wolf

50 — 75 Dialogues: Gianni Pettena and Robert Smithson

76 — 97 Dialogues: Gianni Pettena and Allan Kaprow

98 — 107 Dialogues: Gianni Pettena and Gordon Matta-Clark

108 — 119 Dialogues: Emanuele Piccardo and Gianni Pettena

120 — 127 Dialogues: Emanuele Piccardo and Fabio Sargentini

128 — 169 Superarchitettura Italy 1963-1973:
Gianni Pettena
UFO
Ugo La Pietra
9999
Pietro Derossi
Superstudio

Off-Site:
Ingalill Wahlroos-Ritter

Beyond Environment is, appropriately, a project that is presented in multiple platforms and range of media: a publication, a symposium, a design competition, a book launch at the 2014 Venice Biennale and an exhibition of multiple artifacts that includes video, photographs and textual reproductions; appropriate in that the original projects produced by Gianni Pettena and his collaborators were direct provocations to the conventional production and presentation of art and architectural artifacts. As Bruno Orlandoni observes in his introduction to this volume, the work showcased in *Beyond Environment* can be reevaluated through our contemporary lens on multiple levels. From Pop Art to Land Art, from material specificity to environmental atmosphere, from political experimentation to formal discovery, the richness of this art-architecture complex is astonishing. Of particular pleasure in examining these original projects is finding deep and meaningful connections between the exhibited work and contemporary tendencies that influence architectural agendas.

With careful consideration and construction, the richness and variety of the projects presented in *Beyond Environment* point to a historically significant range of provocations that constitute fundamental elements of the education of an architect: urban interventions that catalyze social and political change;[1] multi-disciplinary collaborations and Happenings of fleeting immediacy that presage current trends in socially responsible public art and architecture of civic engagement;[2] environmentally multivalent installations, precursors to architecture with sophisticated atmospheric nuances and sustainable subtexts;[3] materially specific experiments that bring to mind innovative practices in applied materials research;[4] and most significantly, works of art and architecture with off-site and on-site manifestations, echoing the words and work of Robert Smithson, Rosalind Krauss, and Miwon Kwon. Building on theories of post-medium specific art and architecture, the multivalent presentations that constitute *Beyond Environment* provide rich fodder for proliferating these discussions, off-site, and in Hollywood.

WUHO, the Woodbury University Hollywood Outpost, is a gallery associated with a school of architecture. Many schools of architecture have galleries associated with them. What makes WUHO unique is it's off-site location. Located on the storied Walk of Fame in Hollywood, 10 miles from the suburban fabric surrounding the primary campus in Burbank and 150 miles from

1 Gianni Pettena's *Carabinieri* finds particular resonance in the work of muf architecture/art.

2 UFO's urban Happenings are progenitors to the political provocations collected in Suzanne Lacy's *Mapping Terrain: New Genre Public Art* (Seattle, Wash: Bay Press, 1995).

3 See, for example, the emphasis on environments and atmospheric multi-media effects in Sylvia Lavin's *Kissing Architecture* (Princeton, N.J: Princeton University Press, 2011) and the landscape pieces of Andrea Zittel, reminiscent of Ugo La Pietra's immersive environments.

4 Gianni Pettena's *Ice Houses* are relevant in the context of innovative material research such as that described in Sheila Kennedy's *Material Misuse* (London: Architectural Association Publications, 2001) as well as the work of Toshiko Mori and the play she makes in her projects of immaterial and hyper material effects.

5 Piccardo and Wolf use the term Superarchitecture in relation to the *Superarchitettura* exhibitions (1966-1967), organized by Superstudio and Archizoom, as well as to the coursework offered by Leonardo Savioli in 1967— a point of convergence for the protagonists of architectural experimentation in the 1960s and 1970s in Florence.

the industrial landscape of the secondary campus in San Diego, this 15' wide storefront is immediately and idiosyncratically flanked by a Smoke Shop to the north and the Cupcake Theater to the south. This glitzy shabbiness appropriately serves as the backdrop for Emanuele Piccardo and Amit Wolf's *Beyond Environment*. As a site of architectural education, WUHO showcases architecture's myriad forms, from exhibitions and symposia to interactive and virtual projects, videos, photographs, drawings, mock-ups, prototypes, and environmental installations.

Admittedly WUHO has also hosted several *superarchitetture*.[5] In 2011, architect Jennifer Bonner overflowed the gallery with 3300 gallons of water, echoing the 9999 group and its 1971 *S-Space Festival* at the Space-Electronic discotheque in Florence. Anya Sirota's inhabitable drawing, *The Beta Movement* (2011), unquestionably evokes Pettena's interventions at San Giovanni Valdarno, with its bold graphic striations and the reuses it makes of urban contexts. The 2010 installation *Stay Down Champion Stay Down*, by Molly Hunker and Greg Corso, more than suggests Allan Kaprow's *Fluids* and the rediscovered *Record II*, with their stacking/rupturing techniques, atmospheric glow, and formal fluidity. While the subject of the *Beyond Environment* exhibition is the series of environments produced by Pettena in collaboration with Kaprow, Smithson and others, the gallery provides a resonant subtext in a venue that emphasizes process over artifact, interactivity over subjectivity, collaboration over individuality, and situational ephemeras over fixed contexts.

Ingalill Wahlroos-Ritter

Associate Dean, Woodbury School of Architecture
Director, WUHO

Introduction:
Bruno Orlandoni

Whoever was working in and around Superarchitecture at the time — today we would say in "real time"— cannot be but enthusiastic to learn that in the last ten years the movement has again attracted the attention of critics, including Emanuele Piccardo and Amit Wolf. There is a great deal of pleasure and curiosity in discovering how this phenomenon is reevaluated in other ways and following other approaches, revisiting the categories once used so as to view them with new eyes. *Beyond Environment* challenges what Paola Navone and myself did right (and what we missed) forty years ago. It is probably a good time to reopen the question — half a century has not passed in vain — and put some order among the similar but different disciplines of architecture and art, rediscovering unknown or underestimated connections and relationships. Removing irregular participants of the movement, for instance architects that were drawn into the centrifugal history of the *Superarchitettura* but certainly today must be considered through a different lens, is only a first step; identifying imitators, followers, and attendant successors a second step.

I would like to point out only a few of the potential venues that are still open for research. First, the issue of the relationship between the varied architects and groups addressing cityscape and landscape, architecture and urban planning, and, in a stricter sense, the impact of one on the other. Piccardo's *Radical city* in Turin (2012) broached similar issues as it insisted on the unassailable importance of the piazza and the discotheque.[1] Similarly, Piccardo's and Wolf's recent contributions to the rethinking of the UFO group, the third to emerge from the *Superarchitettura* events after Superstudio and Archizoom, posited UFO's privileged theoretical position in the debate around visual meaning and semiotics.[2] The effort to continue these explorations by cutting across the question of environment and the links between Land Art, Performance Art and Superarchitecture appear a truly productive one.

Since its inception, from Archigram to Raimund Abraham to Hans Hollein and Walter Pichler, architectural experimentalism and its anti-utopian megastructures have dealt with the question of landscape. This strand of work has been able to provide a continuous stream of universalizing if radical visions for the field: *Alles ist arkitektur.* It is not a coincidence that Superarchitecture's closest references within the visual arts were recuperated from Pop Art and from Land Art. I recall Adolfo Natalini, sitting in his hyper-decorated studio, confessing with no trouble that both his

1 Emanuele Piccardo, curator, *Radical City*, May 30 to June 30, 2012, at the Archivio di Stato di Torino, Turin.

2 Emanuele Piccardo, "Sperimentare la parodia nello spazio pubblico," and Amit Wolf, "Lezioni di sperimentalismo teorico," *UFO Story: Dall'architettura radicale al design globale;* Stefano Pezzato Ed. [Centro per L'arte Contemporanea Luigi Pecci – Prato, 30 Settembre – 3 Febbraio 2013] (Prato, 2012) 16-19, 20-21.

3 Bruno Orlandoni, and Giorgio Vallino, *Dalla città al cucchiaio: saggi sulle nuove avanguardie nell'architettura e nel design* (Torino: Studio Forma, 1977).

Superstudio and Archizoom have been deeply influenced by the Pistoia Pop artists Roberto Barni, Umberto Buscioni, and Gianni Ruffi. Along similar lines, Gianni Pettena has always confessed his debt to Robert Smithson, and this conjecture plays a central role in *Beyond Environment.*

These choices (Pop Art and Land Art) appeared somewhat secondary and conjunctional at the time. The pivotal role played by industrial design and the exchange with the *Milano da Bere* of Florentine immigrants such as Giovanni Michelucci, Leonardo Ricci and Leonardo Savioli and the world of superproduction — not only commercial but also cultural and mediatic — seem now to have been more and more a mistake: a honey trap of events and counter events, starting with the 14th Milan *Triennale,* that would derail and ultimately shorten the movement's lifespan, bringing it to an end.
To me, Pettena`s profound engagements circa 1970 with the question of art and life, environment and affect, stand in contrast to the narrative of 'Radical Design' — the narrative that took possession over the understating of the movement after 1974. Surely, other *superarchitetti* actively pursued a change of direction toward the art world, but the only significant moment along these lines was Alessandro Mendini's architecture section in *Contemporanea,* a large scale exhibition that took place in Rome in the underground parking structure of Villa Borghese.

In 1977 Giorgio Vallino and I chose the statement *Dalla cittá al cucchiaio* as the title of my second — and last in thirty years — foray into the "radical experiments of Italian architecture."[3] I was not only interested in furthering my research with Navone, but also in countering what already seemed like an intention to minimize the movement and its indulgence in industrial design.
The overturning of the Rationalist maxim, to which the title refers, from the city to the fact of design, was perfectly fitting with Emilio Ambasz *Italy: the New Domestic Landscape* (1972, MoMA) and was also in line with its devastating mind set, claiming ownership and usage as the only political actions available in the aftermath of 1969. At the same time, we aimed to point out to the growing risks of what would become Post Modern architecture. Superarchitecture's turn towards industrial design offered many misconceptions as well. First of all, it led to a historical reconsideration of the more developed work of Ettore Sottsass, an outside figure to the movement, as one of its climaxes. Sottsass had certainly been one of the fathers, and among the most important references for the *superarchitetti* because

of his particular mind frame and the cultural/productive platforms he created for the movement, most notably the *Pianeta Fresco* and his division in Sergio Camilli's Poltronova. Sottsass' most significant contribution, however, was a late one — *Metafore*, a forgotten nod to the *superarchitetti*, which was produced in parts between 1972 and 1974 to 1976, and homogeneously published in Italy only in 2002.[4] This can be considered as the most Land Art-inspired of all his works and closest to the movement. But this poetic tribute to Land Art, as it is clear from Piccardo/Wolf's latest efforts, was already eclipsed in 1971-72 by the un-architecture of Pettena and his *Ice Houses.*

4 Ettore Sottsass, Milco Carboni, and Barbara Radice, *Metafore* (Milan: Skira, 2002).

Beyond Environment provides several profound considerations on the relationship between the natural environment, the constructed and deconstructed environment, and the reasons why some of the *superarchitetti* that were working along these lines deserve further scrutiny. Even if we are aware of the transient nature of criticism and history and, in paricular, that of architecture history and criticism, we can state that between 1972 and 1975 the movement was, in many ways, unconsciously or not, clearing a new ground for itself somewhere between the visual arts and industrial design.
Pettena, Ugo La Pietra, and UFO were actively working within the former, oblivious to the reality of high design, while Archizoom, with Andrea Branzi in particular, had a more relevant position in the latter, also thanks to his alliance with the Montefibre and Alessandro Mendini's magazine *Modo. Modo*, like the Superarchitecture, was at first enthusiastic about its radical architectural role, yet progressively turned its attentions to industrial production and design, therefore tracking the gradual disappearance of Italian experimentalism.

The shift towards the production of design follies is also responsible for the historical exclusion of other episodes, important in the context of Pettena's art-architecture complex. I am thinking of group Cavart's 1975 seminar *Impossible architecture*, which took place in a disused quarry. I can't help but think of the statement of Smithson that, "one would have to work in a quarry or in a mining area", which Pettena recorded in 1972, and is also quoted in this book.
And I can't help but think of the work the American un-architect Gordon Matta-Clark and his 1974-1975 *Splitting* and *Conical Intersect*. Matta-Clark's use of the term un-architecture is continuous with Pettena. Still the American's drilling, boring, and dissecting operations, treating architecture as if it was a geologic rather than manmade agent and ground, is particularly provocative in the context of Smithson's Land Art and Pettena's un-architecture, and

their use of derelict environments. Such geological-manmade dialectics, I would propose, are at the heart of this publication.

∧ 15
UFO
Installation
at XIV Triennale
Milan, 1968
Marcatrè 41/42
1968

From the City to the Environment: Emanuele Piccardo

"There were two aspects of Smithson's work which I was interested in: his ability to understand the environment and the way he reproduced this in his works; and his more conscious, rather than unconscious, close interest in the events concerning architecture."[1]

1 Gianni Pettena, "Conversation a Salt lake City", *Domus* 516 (1972): 53-55.

This impression was confirmed when Gianni Pettena, Lawrence Alloway and Robert Smithson went to Salt Lake City to see *Spiral Jetty*. The pictures of the spiral distributed by the Dawn Gallery did not allow a correct interpretation of it, as they were lacking of scale, nonetheless it was important to have a direct contact with the context, entering inside the spiral and then getting out of it and looking at it in its place. In fact, Smithson made also an aerial film of the work, in order to make it more comprehensible and emphasize its large scale and the strong impact in the landscape around. It is certainly not the case that Pettena defines this work as architecture, even if the different approach comes out in the conversation he made with Smithson at Salt Lake City for the magazine Domus in 1972.

"[...] I would say mainly in Europe — Smithson writes — one would have to work in a quarry or in a mining area, because everything is so cultivated in terms of Church or aristocracy [...] I agree about that, thinking about the distinction you made between here and Europe — Pettena replies — [...] Here, let's say you've got a lot of land and they there don't [...] I think I understand why you prefer dismissed areas rather than untouched areas. But the fact is that for me those areas are still too natural [...] I have no right to touch a natural area and an old disused mine it's a place that nature recycled according to it's standard, thus subtracting it to me [...] I think you have to find a site that is free of scenic meaning-Smithson replies. Scenery has too many built-in meanings [...] I'm thinking that perhaps you are able to do something in a town in Europe-Pettena

2 ibidem.

3 The birthplace of the *Superarchitettura* was Florence. In 1966 Superstudio and Archizoon were born. In 1967 the UFO group was born too, while in 1968 Gianni Pettena and 1999 (becoming 9999 in 1970) started their activity. Zziggurat followed. Pietro Derossi was active in Turin since 1966, and Carlo Giammarco, together with Giorgio Ceretti, Riccardo Rosso and Maurizio Vogliazzo founded Gruppo Strum in 1972. Ugo La Pietra worked in Milan since 1966.

again replies-while you are not able to do something in a town here [...]"[2]

Following this dialogue one can easily understand the deep differences. On one side Smithson acts in the natural context, as it has been modified by nature and man's work (the abandoned mines), on the other Pettena acts in the urban context, the way it is after nature has altered it, so nature acts as architecture does.

My research starts from this clash of ideas in defining the environment to investigate the relationship between Italy and the United States in the decade of the Sixties-Seventies. In Italy the environment is urban; it is the public space of the *piazza* and the discotheque, the public space for entertainment par excellence. In fact, every single artist/architect belonging to the new avant-garde movement of Italian architecture, *Superarchitettura*, has designed at least one discotheque.[3] In the States, on the contrary, artists shift from the inside close environment of an art gallery to the happening taking place in the outside open environment without any walls and rooms. It is crucial though to distinguish between artists like Allan Kaprow, who experimented the developments of the happening in the open spaces, with the help of students-performers, and the land artists acting in a solitary way, without any audience, in the landscape. The difference between the concept of environment in Italy and the United States is witnessed by the work of Gianni Pettena, who worked in both countries. His focus between 1968 and 1972 was to point out the critical state of the city, emphasizing in a provocative way the relationship between space (the abstract concept of space) and public (both the public space of a square or building, and the public audience).
In fact, the political scene of 1968 and the students' movement had naturally influenced his Italian projects and also the ones of Ugo La Pietra and the UFO.

The American works of Pettena, were free of those boundaries but still inside of the urban areas, a typical feature of his theoretical research, and expressed autonomous forms and languages, without any reference to the land artists whom he knew, but who were so far from him. In order to understand the meaning and birth of the environment as I am using the term, it is necessary to make one step beyond, and talk of the experience of the German artist Kurt Schwitter, and one of the first environments ever conceived, that he made in his house in Hannover in 1924.

> "[...] Called Column or Cathedral of Erotic Misery — Michael Kirby writes — its walls and ceilings were covered solidly with angled and protruding abstract shapes. There were recessed lights, secret-sliding panels [...]"[4]

4 See Michael Kirby, *Happening*, (New York: E.P. Dutton&Co, 1968) 22.

This shows how the avant-gardes (Dada and Futurism) had already expressed the same alterations of the boundaries between the disciplines, which forty years later Kaprow reproduced in his works: new variations on the same theme.
It is impossible to understand the different definitions of environment, between urban and natural landscape, without analyzing the cultural background in the Sixties in general and in particular the Italian situation and its relationship with the International political-cultural scene in England and the United States. It is possible to draw a line between the research in Italy and the United States that combines the theoretical-political approach of the *piazza,* and partly the discotheque, that were the concern of the artists Gianni Pettena, Ugo La Pietra and UFO; and the theoretical approach of the happening that was moving from the environment (inside) to the environment (outside) in the American works of Pettena, Robert Smithson, Allan Kaprow and Gordon Matta-Clark.

The American context is culturally virgin and lacks an historical background, but it is rich with void places, like lakes, forests and the deserts, in which the artists could build a background theory. In Europe, on the contrary, the cultural background dates back centuries, and it is a part of people's minds, and sometimes is too heavy a burden with its history. All these assumptions make us understand why the Europeans tend to deconstruct and dematerialize history, while the Americans go the opposite way, complicating, and consequently defining the background where to act, as they already possess a nearly infinite space of continental land.

Superarchitettura Italy 1963-1973

The students'sit-ins at the Universities of both continents emphasized the creative role of the Architecture schools in Italy (Milan, Turin and Rome) since 1963 and at Berkeley, California, with the Free Speech Movement in 1964. The protest had a cultural background. On one side there was the crisis of outdated didactic programs, which no longer followed the evolution of society in the Sixties with its deep change of tastes and the mass culture.
On the other side, the end of the Modern movement took place, after its decline started during the Fifties and the newly born Team X and New Brutalism, both inspired by Alison and Peter Smithson. This was the cultural, social and political background of the birth of the *Superarchitettura*. The overcoming of the discipline of architecture shifted the theory toward new media, like video and photography that broke the boundaries between architecture and other disciplines, like art, music, literature, cinema and theater. Several movie directors influenced the new generations and the radical architects too. Just think of Stanley Kubrick (*Lolita*, 1962; *2001: A Space Odyssey*, 1968), Michelangelo Antonioni (*Red Desert*, 1964; *Blow up*,1966; *Zabriskie Point*, 1970), François Truffaut (*The 400 blows*,1959; *Fahrenheit 451*,1966) and Jean-Luc Godard (*Breathless*,1960; *Contempt*,1963). Everything mixed up and it was hard to recognize what was the artists' work and what the architects'.

The *Superarchitettura* movement consisted of an alternative to the dominant academic establishment and took its inspiration from the sit-ins in the Campus of Berkeley and the hippy and human rights movements.

It occurred primarily in the city of Florence, where most of the *Superarchitetti* were inspired and aimed at the Anglo-Saxon world. The Archigram in fact were born in Great Britain in the Sixties following the theories of Buckminster Fuller. In Austria too the *Superarchitettura* had a great impact with the work of Haus Rucker-Co, Coop Himmelblau, Hans Hollein and Walter Pichler. A few months after the flooding of Florence in 1966 the first two radical groups were born: Archizoom and Superstudio.

> "The pictures taken during the flooding portray a different Florence, and give a very different vision of the historical view of the city — Toraldo di Francia writes — showing us a city with stone feet and surface. It is Florence, with its monuments immersed in a slimy fluid, dense with naphtha... a dynamic situation, which immediately separated the architecture box of the monuments from its basement, so that the tectonics was debated by these pictures. It became an iconic image for a series of operations on culture in general, trying to overturn the traditional inherited values that did not satisfy anymore the economical and social system."[5]

5 See Cristiano Toraldo di Francia, in Emanuele Piccardo, "Dopo la rivoluzione. Azioni e protagonisti dell'architettura radicale italiana1963-1973" (Busalla: plug_in, 2009) DVD.

6 See Cristiano Toraldo di Francia, "Verso la liberazione dalle Archimanie", *TAO* 13 (2012): 19.

In the same year, 1966, the two groups made explicit their theories organizing the exhibition *Superarchitettura*, at Galleria d'arte Jolly 2 in Pistoia, whose manifesto already made clear the influence of pop culture: "*Superarchitettura* is the architecture of superproduction, of superconsumption, of superpersuasion to consume, of the supermarket, of the superman and of premium petrol."

> "Since the first operation — Toraldo di Francia writes — consisting of the occupation of a whole art gallery with self-built objects of an uncertain use, between furniture, and architecture model or sculpture, we had stated the crisis of the equation "form follows function". We wanted to stress the importance of the symbolic function, and the tactile experience deriving from the use of the objects, which we deconstructed on purpose, to stimulate a dismantling perception that was to create new and alternative uses of them."[6]

The idea of dismantling the structure of objects was not only a reference for Archizoom and Superstudio, who had designed armchairs, sofas, lamps, etc., since their beginning, and eventually moved to a more theoretic dimension with their projects *Monumento Continuo* and *No Stop City*, but also for other *Superarchitetti* who

considered the city-object as the place for experimentation their theories. That was why the public space, the *piazza*, was chosen as the best environment in which to dismantle the structure of habits, with the aim of breaking up the establishment with powerful happenings. The political influence of what happened in 1968 *in piazza* was evident in the works of the *Superarchitects* Pettena, La Pietra and UFO, but also in all the artists of that period.
Pettena started his italian research with the trilogy *Carabinieri*, *Milite Ignoto* and *Grazia&Giustizia,* all made in 1968.

> "The trilogy was also a reflection of the desire to transcribe thoughts in terms of slogans, typical of the student revolt in May 1968; the desire expressed but to no effect, to spell out an ideological position, to signal the intention to take a stand, even as operators in the field of architecture."[7]

Pettena's use of gigantic cardboard letters is meant for self-destruction, and it put in evidence the presence-absence of the artwork, that also symbolizes the presence-absence of institutions. The work was set in a public place to create a dialogue breaking with stereotypes, like the students did at Berkeley by placing the script People Park in 1964.[8]
In order to understand the power of Pettena's message, we should think of his most symbolic work, *Grazia&Giustizia,* titled after the name of the Italian Ministry of Justice. He bravely made it in Palermo, where the power mafia was overwhelming the institutions during the Sixties.

> "The large letters were carried in a long procession to the sea and, accompanied by the musicians of the group Musica Elettronica Viva, playing as if at a funeral in New Orleans, were thrown into the water, where they slowly became soaked and sank."[9]

Pettena occupied the public space when the Florentine group UFO[10] made the first happenings, and precisely with the group of Lapo Binazzi, he participated to the 6th Masaccio Prize in San Giovanni Valdarno with the work *Dialogo con Arnolfo.*
It consisted of a transformation of the medieval palace made by

7 See Stefania Coppi Pettena, *Gianni Pettena* (Milan: Silvana Editoriale, 2003) 148.

8 People Park is a public park made by the Berkeley students in 1964 on the grounds of the University. For many years it had remained neglected, until the students protested against the commercial use of it and this led to a transformation of the area.

9 See note 7.

10 The group UFO was founded in 1967 by Lapo Binazzi, Riccardo Foresi, Titti Maschietto, Carlo Bachi, Patrizia Cammeo and Sandro Gioli (only until 1968), inside the Faculty of Architecture of the University of Florence. Massimo Giovannini and Mario Spinella joined it only in 1968. It is considered to be the group of the "radical" Italian experimentation because of their events disturbing the rituals and miths of social and urban contemporary life.
They intended to turn architecture into a show, transforming it into an event, an action of urban and ecological guerrilla.

Arnolfo di Cambio, using a diagonal black and silver stripe surface to close the ground floor loggia, which caused a physical and perceptive cancellation of it. He anticipated what happened later in the United States with his *Ice House I*, *Ice House II* and *Clay House*. Modifying the perception of the architecture object is a recurring theme in his work, and it is a part of the broader concept of dismantling of the structure of a pre-existing language. He aimed at creating a new and autonomous language, clashing with the old and disrupting the iconography.

In the same context, *6th Masaccio Prize*, UFO made the *Superurbeffimero n.7* a series of actions and performances in the same way of the Allan Kaprow's happenings like *18 Happenings in 6 parts*.[11] The UFO were influenced by the presence of Umberto Eco at the Faculty of Architecture in Florence (1966-1969), who was teaching Decoration class, and acted in the urban environment with the *Urboeffimeri* — inflatable objects made of polyethylene that gave new visual outlines to the space. They were also used as a protection against the police charging the student during the protests, or as communication media: *Colgate con Vietcong*, a criticism toward the American war in Vietnam, represented by the Colgate toothpaste, with a Vietcong inside as a free gift; and *Potele agli studenti*,[12] mocking an improbable slogan pronounced with an Italian-Chinese accent. In their works the UFO suggested a new criticism of our key collective imagery using the happening as a source of reflections on theory and behavior, they were keen on unofficial information and aimed at inventing new keys to understand social and political issues.

During the decade 1960-1970, there was a strong need to experiment new ways of using public urban spaces and also ones 'own body, as it happened in Como with *Campo Urbano* in 1969, curated by Luciano Caramel:

> "[...] that meant to bring the artist into direct relationship with the community of an urban area and the places of everyday life... Therefore, nothing special was commissioned to the participants [...]"[13]

Campo Urbano was the most important urban collective show of that time, the chief protagonists in the art experimentations were invited: Bruno Munari, Gianni Colombo, Giuseppe Chiari (Fluxus),

11 In the fall of 1959 the Society Reuben & Kaprow sent a letter out to a big group of people in New York writing about the 18 happenings that were going to take place and inviting to participate with the artist Allan Kaprow. The Reuben gallery also sent two kinds of official invitations, in one there were plastic bags containing photographies, wood, painted fragmants and cut figures. In the other they explained that they gallery space was divided in three rooms with collages and video projections on the walls and gave the dates and schedule.

12 The *Urboeffimero* occupied the space, invaded it and then disappeared in the crowd of the students` movement, becoming its icon, and underlining the importance of the actions against the power. The concept of the use of the artwork expressed in the book *Opera Aperta* by Umberto Eco (1962) is the fundamental idea under the *Urboeffimeri*. Eco considered that each time an artwork was used was also interpreted, and the work is revised under an original perspective.

13 Luciano Caramel, Bruno Munari, Ugo Mulas (curated by) *Campo Urbano* (Como: Editrice Cesare Nani, 1969) 1.

14 Tommaso Trini, "Il sistema disequilibrante", Ugo La Pietra. *Abitare la città* (Torino: Allemandi, 2010) 62.

Giulio Paolini, Luciano Fabro, Enrico Baj, Grazia Varisco, Gianni Emilio Simonetti, Davide Boriani, Gabriele De Vecchi... For the first time the artists compared one with the other without any limits and using no readymade objects for the purpose, as it used to be in art gallery shows in the past. The *piazza* is the location where the action took place, in that same city, as Giuseppe Terragni renovated it, the most revolutionary among the fascist architects.
Campo urbano has been the one and only confrontation between Gianni Pettena, Ugo La Pietra and the other Italian artists.
Pettena burst in the place uninvited with his work *Laundry*, underwear, t-shirts and bed sheets that represented a public washing hanging from one side to the other of the Cathedral's square.
With this work, Pettena intended to undermine the importance of the religious and political power. In the same context Ugo La Pietra, with his *Copro una strada e ne faccio un'altra,* built a wooden triangular structure covered with black cellophane that redesigned a pedestrian road, creating a change of perception in the urban space and a sense of physical *détournement* in the viewers.
In the same year, 1969, La Pietra theorized *Il Sistema Disequilibrante,* an experimentation with new languages that were to give that sense of alteration, exactly like it had happened in *Immersioni:*

> "[...] these invite us to get out of the surrounding context, but they replicate themselves to become almost claustrophobic, and offer a different background – Tommaso Trini writes – but they deny it is the only, absolute option, and recover and impose some disalienating values in disguise of separation [...]"[14]

The desire was to get out of normal psychological restraints and loose the balance following new patterns of behavior in space.
La Pietra's best art performance in the urban environment was *Il commutatore*, in the suburbs of Milan: using an inclined board, to lean on and observe the city from different angles and perspectives, he created a situation that was to give a different perception of the city. The lack of balance is again the theme that the artist brought to the Triennale in 1968, as he aimed at plunging the audience into new behavior patterns using an audio-video environment.
The difference with the environments of Kaprow was the lack of a program for the happening, as it was the audience's involvement that alone made the happening itself.

The relationship between space, user and senses was in fact the main theme of the architect Leonardo Savioli's readings for his class of Furniture & Interior Design at the Faculty of Architecture in Florence in 1967. His assistants Adolfo Natalini (Superstudio), Paolo Deganello (Archizoom), Maurizio Sacripanti, Pietro Derossi (Gruppo Strum) Giancarlo and Francesco Capolei (the designers of the discotheque Piper in Rome 1965) convinced him to add to his interests the discotheque, considered to be one of the places of sensory involvement.[15]

The *Superarchitetti* considered the discotheque a real architecture, and designed *É la fine del mondo* in Turin in 1966 by Pietro Derossi (with Giorgio Ceretti), *Mach2* by Superstudio in 1967 and *Space Electronic* by gruppo 9999 in 1969 — both in Florence — and in the same year Ugo La Pietra designed the discotheque *Bang Bang* with its boutique *Altre Cose* in Milan. The UFO used to stage their parody of cartoons in the discotheque *Bamba Issa # 1 and # 2* in Forte dei Marmi (1969-1972).[16] The disco was considered one of the environments for happenings, like the theatre staged by Carmelo Bene and the Living Theatre, art exhibitions of Arte Povera and open discussions.

The *S-Space Festival* organized by group 9999 (that in the meantime had changed its original name 1999) in 1971 at the *Space Electronic* with the Superstudio is one example. UFO, Superstudio, Zziggurat, Ugo La Pietra, Gianni Pettena, Remo Buti, Renato Ranaldi and the English group Street Farmer all took part in this event, where close circuit monitors were installed and broadcasting a video inspired by Saint Francis' *Cantico delle Creature*, emphasizing a life in connection with nature.[17] The ecological approach of group 9999 during the festival was not only theoretical, but also practical. In fact, the ground floor of the Space Electronic had been flooded with water, and a *Vegetable Garden House* for fresh greens was growing on the first floor. The group 9999 won MoMA's *Competition for Young Designers* with its project the *Vegetable Garden House* included in MoMA's exhibition *Italy: the new domestic landscape* curated by Emilio Ambasz in 1972.

15 "The space is not a definitive image, a symbol, a type, but it becomes an image evoking, pretending, and therefore it can be placed at different consuming levels from the user". See Leonardo Savioli, Adolfo Natalini, "Lo spazio di coinvolgimento", *Casabella* 326 (1968): 32.

16 In the discotheque they choose camels and sand together with a papier maché scenery to decor, after a parody of the cartoon *Paperino e la clessidra magica*, Topolino n.25, 1951. See Emanuele Piccardo, "UFO Sperimentare la parodia nello spazio pubblico," *UFO Story. Dall'architettura radicale al design globale* (Prato: Centro per l'arte contemporanea Pecci, 2012) 18.

17 "Our existence depends only on living creatures that we know and do not know: the nature. The light and the capital fade and loose their importance, becoming mediums again". Technology was used at the beginning by the group 9999 as a medium between mankind and nature, "born to protect the man, it first hit nature and now rebels against man". See *9999, S-Space Festival*, (Firenze: 9999, 1972) 254.

American Environment: from Inside to Outside

This way of occupying and using an inside environment showed the differences between the concept of environment for the Italians and the Americans.
The discotheque is certainly the environment that contrasted most with the idea of environment of Allan Kaprow's *18 happenings in six parts* and his following happenings, as it is not an art gallery, but a space of emotional involvement.
In the United States there were many different approaches to the concept of environment. We would point out here the difference between the theoretical approach of Kaprow and the one of Smithson — while Matta-Clark had a different physical and conceptual approach from both of them and only superficially similar to the one of Pettena.

Kaprow was a painter, later became a sculptor, and approached the happenings in the outside environment only later on.
He followed the Bauhaus theatre, the Dada experience, and put on stage everyday life aspects in line with John Cage's earlier performances.[18] It was 1921, at the time of the *found environment* that actions started to take place in the outside environment: André Breton invited the Dadaists, but the result had been too theatrical, in spite of the structure of unpredictability.
Unpredictability decreased its importance, also for Kaprow, who started to give precise scripts to his performers in order to achieve a certain rhythm out of them.
At the beginning, the public was passive during his happenings; later, after he made them more engaging for the people, and that was like proposing to go out of a tunnel, which had became more and more claustrophobic.

When Kaprow got out and worked in the outside environment, he stopped working with artists, poets and friends and started to work with students and a performer public, as in, for example *Household* and *Fluids*, among the most interesting of his works.

18 John Cage, during his conversation with Michael Kirby and Michael Schechner, replied to the question *What's your definition of theatre?* as follows: "I would simply say that theatre is something which engages both the eye and the ear-Cage writes – The two public senses are seeing and hearing; the senses of taste, touch, and odor are more proper to intimate, nonpublic, situations. The reason I want to make my definition of theatre that simple is so one could view everyday life itself as theatre..." This answer underlines the importance of the happening in everyday life, in spite of stating an improvised program, as the whole of Cage's work demonstrates, and in part also the one of Kaprow's. See Mariellen R.Sandford, *Happenings and other acts*, (London: Routledge, 1995) 43.

In *Household*, 1964, students at Cornell University were the performers and protagonists. They were divided into two groups, separating men from women and the piece consisted of twelve actions, one after the other, following the program written by Kaprow. These "improvisations" took a different time dimension in the outside environment, without any spatial limits.
Fluids took place in Pasadena and Los Angeles in 1967 it was a single event and it consisted of building a rectangular volume of ice using sea salt as binding agent. People who spontaneously replied to an advertisement hung at the Pasadena Art Museum built the structure. The similarities with Gianni Pettena's *Ice Houses* and *Fluids* are clearly evident, not only for the use of the same material — ice — but also conceptually speaking: both made a structure apparently without any meaning, and rapidly deteriorating because of the fluid state, that expressed its real meaning of nothingness, void, evaporating under the sun light.

> "The structures indicate no significance. In fact, their very blankness and their rapid deterioration proclaims the opposite of significance [...] Fluids is in a state of continuous fluidity and there's literally nothing left but a puddle of water — and that evaporates. If you want to pursue the metaphor further, it is a comment on urban planning and planned obsolescence [...]"[19]

But this statement is in contradiction with what comes out in the dialog between Kaprow and Smithson concerning "What is a Museum?"[20]

> "I'm interested for the most part in what's not happening, that area between events which could be called the gap — Smithson writes — This gap exists in the blank and void regions or settings that we never look at. A museum devoted to different kinds of emptiness could be developed.
> The emptiness could be defined by the actual installation of art."[21]

While Kaprow replies ironically, that if one speaks realistically:

19 See Mariellen R. Sandford, *Happenings and other acts*, (London: Routledge, 1995) 187-188.

20 See Jack Flam, *Robert Smithson: The collected writings*, (Los Angeles: University of California Press, 1996) 43-51.

21 ibidem 44.

22 ibidem 48.

23 ibidem 271.

24 ibidem 178.

> "[...] you'll never get anybody to put up the dough for a mausoleum, a mausoleum to emptiness, to nothing though it might be the most poetic statement of your position. You'll never get anyone to pay for the Guggenheim to stay empty all year [...]"[22]

When Kaprow made *Fluids*, he was very close to Smithson's ideas on emptiness and indefiniteness: certainly a significant contradiction between theory and action. Robert Smithson, on the other hand, did not practice happenings and, since the beginning, had a peculiar relationship with the natural environment.

> "[...] When I was about seven I did very large paper constructions of dinosaurs which in a way — writes Smithson — I suppose, relate right up to the present in terms of the film I made on The *Spiral Jetty* — the prehistoric motif runs throughout the film [...]"[23]

While most artists were showing their works in art galleries, Smithson already had a different theoretical approach to the *site* and to the *non-site* in a relational dialectic between the inside and outside.

> "[...] The site, in a sense, is the physical, raw reality — the earth or the ground that we are really not aware of when we are in an interior room or studio or something like that — and so I decided that I would set limits in terms of this dialogue (it's a back and forth rhythm that goes between indoors and outdoors), and as a result I went and instead of putting something on the landscape I decided it would be interesting to transfer the land indoors, to the nonsite, which is an abstract container. This summer I went out west and selected sites — physical sites — that in a sense are part of my art. I went to a volcano and collected a ton of lava and sent it back to New York and that was set up in my non-site interior limit [...]"[24]

Smithson's attitude in his relationship with the environment is explained in his text *Entropy and New Monumentalism* published in 1966 in Artforum:

> "[...] Instead of causing us to remember the past like the old monuments-writes Smithson – the new monuments seem to cause us to forget the future. Instead of being made of natural materials, such as marble, granite, or other kinds of rock, the new monuments are made of artificial materials, plastic, chrome, and electric light. They are not built for the ages, but rather against the ages[...]"[25]

This explains also the use of artificial materials in works like *Asphalt Rundown*, made in Rome in 1969 after the invitation of the art gallery owner Fabio Sargentini, who also organized a solo exhibition of the artist in the gallery *L'Attico*.[26] The invitation came after the Italo-American dancer Simone Forti introduced Sargentini to the New York art gallery owner John Weber.

Asphalt Rundown is a confirmation of what Smithson said to Pettena during their conversation concerning the space where it was worth making his work: a natural abandoned space, at the borders and not in the center, as it had to be *free of any scenical meaning*.[27] The artist dialogued with the place using his language and captured the language expressed by the place, in this case the mine on the *Via Laurentina*, and created a break, a strong gesture, the black, contrasting with the ochre of the tuff in the picture taken by Claudio Abate that created the iconography of the project.
Fabio Sargentini is an important figure because he contributes to know the American artists in Italy. During *Asphalt Rundown* Gianni Pettena met Smithson. The art galleries had been the real school for Pettena, the places where he became an artist and met his friends of the Arte Povera: Mario Merz, Jannis Kounellis, Pino Pascali, Eliseo Mattiacci. As Smithson used to go to museums and art galleries in his youth in New York, also Pettena, who was born in Bolzano 1940, used to go art galleries in Rome and to the Sperone Gallery in Turin. It was thanks to these galleries and to the Forma Gallery in Genoa, active from 1972 to 1982, that continuous exchanges with the United States took place.
The Forma Gallery, founded by Emilio Rebora and Paolo Minetti,

25 ibidem 11.

26 L'Attico was founded in Rome by Fabio Sargentini in 1966. It was a partly underground garage and it changed the concept of art gallery for ever on. The first show at L`Attico was a solo exhibition of Jannis Kounellis, then followed Pino Pascali, Sol Lewitt and Robert Smithson.

27 See note 1.

was the first in 1973 to invite Gordon Matta-Clark to Italy (Genoa) for his project *A W-Hole House.* It consisted of an intervention on a house in the suburbs in the west side of the city, in Sestri Ponente, that was about to be dismantled. Matta-Clark made a square hole in the square roof breaking the symmetry and almost breaking the rules of statics. Zenithal pictures are the only thing left of the work, and photography was part of the work itself. In fact Matta-Clark dissected also the negative films, not only the architecture:

> "[...]I seek typical structures-Matta-Clark writes – which have certain kinds of historical and cultural identities [...] my intervention can transform the structure into an act of communication [...]"[28]

Matta-Clark graduated in Architecture at Cornell University (1964-1968) and, in December 1973, a few months after Pettena published his book *L'Anarchitetto,* he founded the *Anarchitecture group*[29]. This witnesses the relationship between the two artists who were trying to dismantle the structure of architecture and break the limits of the mind, the ethical and artistical limits, with the intention of configuring a new visual and architectural language.

Matta-Clark removed some material, with his cuts, while Pettena was accumulating material, ice (*Ice House*) or clay (*Clay House*), and both changed architecture transforming it into something new. The relationship between the two artists was made stronger not only for the use of the same visual code, and their research aiming to dismantle the existing language through the use of words, but also because they used video and photography as key elements of their performance. These media were not only instruments, but also a real part of the performance itself. Matta-Clark, in particular, confessed his theoretical distance from the California School and Land Art that he shared with Pettena, in his interview with Donald Wall:

> "[...] Land Art is more recent and my break with it is clearer. First, the choice of dealing with either the urban environment in general, and building structures specifically, alters my whole realm of reference and shifts it away from the grand theme of vast natural emptiness which, for the Earth artist, was literally like drawing on a blank

28 Gordon Matta-Clark's Building Dissections, *Arts Magazine* (1976): 74-79.

29 The Anarchitecture group: Laurie Anderson, Joel Fisher, Tina Girouard, Susan Harris, Gen Heighstein, Bernard Kirschenbaum, Richard Landry, Gordon Matta-Clark, Max Newhous, Richard Nonas and Alan Saret. "This term does not imply anti-architecture, but rather is an attempt at clarifying ideas about space which are personal insights and reactions rather than formal socio-political statements" See Gloria Moure, Gordon Matta-Clark. *Works and Collected writings*,(Barcelona: Ediciones Poligrafa, 2006) 369.

canvas... I have chosen not isolation from the social conditions, but to deal directly with social conditions whether by physical implication, as in most of my building works, or through more direct community involvement, which is how I want to see the work develop in the future. I think that differences in context are my primary concern and a major separation from Earth Art [...]"[30]

30 See note 28.

31 Ant Farm was a group of architects, artists and filmakers founded in 1968 by Doug Michels and Chip Lord, and later joined by Curtis Schreier, Hudson Marquez and Dougals Hurr. The inflatable objects were their trademarks, exactly like for UFO. They were produced in 1970 (50x50' Pillow, Spare tire, Clean air pod) and came with an instruction booklet called Inflatecookbook.

Pettena, an American Artist

When Pettena was in the States, he did not reproduce the urgencies of the earthworks, which did not belong to him, but with the help of the students, in Minneapolis and then Salt Lake City, he made a series of actions and performances that recalled the ones of Kaprow in the second half of the Sixties. Kaprow is again a presence, although a background presence, that influenced the actions of many young artists of that time. It is not a coincidence that Chip Lord and Curtis Schreirer, members of the Ant Farm group followed the same strategies of Kaprow in their happenings after the influence of the workshop *Experiments in environments* held by Lawrence Halprin, Anna Halprin and Paul Baum.[31] Anna Halprin, dancer and choreographer, had held her San Francisco Dance's workshops since 1955 and became a point of reference being responsible of transforming dance into performing art.

The Happening as a form of art is in debt to Anna Halprin, as many experimental choreographers like Simone Forti, Trisha Brown and Yvonne Rainer studied at her workshops, as did many artists, performers and composers like Merce Cunningham, Robert Whitman, Robert Morris, La Monte Young, Luciano Berio, John Cage studied there too. All the happenings, dance, environments of American artists were influenced by the theory of the happening of Kaprow to some extent. The environment, urban or natural, art gallery or desert, is the big container of the happenings, of the performing and body art too. This is the context that challenged Gianni Pettena during his art residencies in Minneapolis and Salt Lake City. The beginning of his American adventure has been the project *Wearable Chairs* in April 1971 at the Minneapolis College of Art and Design acting with the students. They were actually "wearing" the chairs, taking them around the city, sitting on a bus, walking in the street, or at the College. His experimentation in Minneapolis too continued with the students, building *Ice House I* and *Ice House II*.

Ice House I was built in an abandoned school inside of a park in Minneapolis in 1971. The building was sprinkled with water all night long and was transformed into a volume of ice. After the transformation was complete, the existing structure was still visible under the transparent ice façade, a clear anticipation of contemporary architecture's features. *Ice House II* was a typical middle class balloon frame house entirely covered with ice to make a cubic volume, and expressed the repetitiveness of this kind of housing development. Nature enters the city in every American work of Pettena, and the same approach he used for *Clay House* and *Tumbleweeds Catcher* in Salt Lake City in 1972. *Clay House* was a middle class white anonymous house that he completely covered with clay, both the façades and the roof, with the help of the students of the University of Utah, in order to change its matter and its anonymous character. Pettena did not change the shape of the building, as he did in Ice House II, but simply acted on its surface and colored it in monochrome dry clay, which cancelled the perception of its depth. The wooden tower of *Tumbleweeds Catcher* belongs to the same concept of the nature entering inside the city. The tumbleweeds are parts of plants growing in the dry climates of the desert, which are blown by the wind and roll for hundreds of miles. Using these Pettena was thinking of a typical American landscape feature.

The last work he made in Salt Lake is *Red Line*, from 1972, the last one of the trilogy, and more similar to his Italian works.
For this happening, he first drew a red line on the city's map marking the borders of the municipality, and then he materially drew it on the road driving a pick-up for the 45 km of the perimeter, acting out a very strong conceptual material gesture with deep spiritual meanings. While Kaprow sometimes used students and sometimes the public, Pettena was always taking advantage of the students-performers' help, and this is certainly a difference between the two artists. At the same time, this happening reminds us of Ugo La Pietra's *La Conquista dello Spazio*, Milan 1971, when he drew a series of white lines on the road symbolizing the conquering

of new spaces for new functions, a powerful action aiming to destabilize the political system and the order of urban grid. Pettena's works in Minneapolis and Salt Lake City represented a meditation on the relationship between the city and the actually residing in it, between homologation of residential architecture and the breaking with space and language using natural materials, like clay and water. The only non-urban encounter of Pettena with nature is witnessed in his photography *About non conscious architecture* (1972-1973). The topic was the unconscious architecture of the structures made by nature in places like the Monument Valley or the Canyon de Chelly. He put together a series of fragments of monumental rocks — the same of the West pioneers' movies, or in the photography of Timothy O' Sullivan and Ansel Adams, portraying the mud huts of Native Americans, and the mines of Great Salt Lake.

The End of Superarchitettura

In 1972 the *Superarchitettura* was celebrated at the MoMA with the exhibition *Italy: the new domestic landscape*, curated by the architect Emilio Ambasz. Pettena refused the invitation to participate, in order to display his work at the prestigious John Weber Gallery. Artforum reviewed the show underlining the powerful conceptual aspect of the works.[32] At the MoMA exhibition there were designers, such as Joe Colombo, Gae Aulenti and Mario Bellini mixed up with counter-designers, such as Archizoom, Superstudio, La Pietra, 9999 and Strum, and the final result lacked of sense.
These counter-designers aimed at breaking the traditional relationship between design and the object, the lamps and sofas they designed were devoted to new spatial behaviors.[33] Superstudio, Archizoom, 9999 and Strum also made some environments with the same features of the discotheque, using sometimes more technology, and set against an artistic backdrop that was abandoned long before: the inside environment.
Pettena understood that the Radical Architecture was not anymore an avant-garde, and predicted that it soon might end. This is what actually happened in 1973 with the utopia of Global Tools (a sort of Arts&Crafts William Morris school).
The only way the Superarchitecture could be saved from decline was acting outside of architecture and starting to work with art, but

32 Gianni Pettena, Italian artist, *Artforum* June (1972) 80-81.

33 Just think of the *Passiflora* lamp designed by Superstudio, or the *Superonda* sofa of Archizooom, the *MGM* and *Dollar* lamps of UFO and the textiles globes of La Pietra, as well as the *Pratone* of Pietro Derossi.

this did not happen. The Radicals could not use their experience in the urban space in their professional life as architects.

There were many reasons why this happened, and they were not all connected to the Radicals' attitude themselves. It was only with the next generation of architects Koolhaas, Tschumi, Hadid, Piano and Rogers, that the avant-garde theories in architecture were implied, but certainly without a formal recognition of their importance.

The failure in the reform of the profession of the architect, at the base of the Cultural Revolution in the Sixties, is witnessed by the quick rise and fall of the Global Tools. In their first meeting Pettena had been portrayed holding a sign with written "Io sono la spia" — "I am the spy" — on it. Spy meant traitor of architecture, even if he was a presence-absence on the scene, never denied his studies. All his works were architecture that he made in an urban context, and using a more artistic language he had marked the real theoretic change since his American travels up to today.

Λ 35
Gianni Pettena
Io sono la spia
Casabella, Milan 1973

Λ 36
Giulio Paolini
Et. quid.amab.nisi.quod aenigma est? Homage to De Chirico's portrait
Campo urbano, Como 1969

Λ 37
Edilio Alpini
Davide Boriani
Gianni Colombo
Gabriele De Vecchi
Tempo libero
Campo urbano, Como 1969

The Education of an Un-Architect: Amit Wolf

The progenitor of the Happening, artist and educator Allan Kaprow has made a career of his obsessions with the de-structuring of art and life with the figure of the un-artist.[1] After first gaining notoriety in New York's art scene with his 1958 *Environment*, he went on to attract attention with site-specific performances, starting with *18 happenings in 6 parts* (1959), segments of which are now reproduced at Los Angeles Contemporary Exhibitions for *Beyond Environment*. Funded by the Graham Foundation, *Beyond Environment* explores contractual, electroacoustic, and video aspects of Kaprow's Happenings, alongside a forgotten collection of drawings by Robert Smithson created in preparation for *Asphalt Rundown* (1969) in Rome. These are supplemented by likewise detailed drawings and images by architect and artist Gianni Pettena, including those of the *Ice Houses* series of the early Seventies. It is important to stress the centrality of architecture in this exhibit. Spanning between Italian Superarchitecture, Happenings, and Land Art, Pettena can be seen as the interlocutor and respondent to art's de-structuring ambitions circa 1970.[2] While running a course parallel but opposed to Kaprow's, with the work (and thought) of Smithson, Pettena embarked on what he terms *anarchitettura* or un-architecture — work that aimed to derail architecture from its professional course by relieving it of its disciplinary formulae and rituals.[3] Pettena met Smithson in Minneapolis in 1971, initiating the development in which Pettena's un-architecture would evolve: from his close readings and critiques of architecture's semiotic turn in the late Sixties to explorations of in-situ pouring and casting; from his transportable urban furniture, measured in meters, to larger and larger settings; from ephemera punctuated by the passing of days to monuments as persistent as the Minnesota winter.

In his essay on Jackson Pollock in the *Art News* of 1958, Allan Kaprow characterized Pollock's singular interaction of visuality and space:

> "Pollock's choice of enormous canvases served many purposes, chief of which for our discussion is that his mural-scale paintings ceased to become paintings and became environments ... We can become entangled in the web to some extent and by moving in and out of the skin of lines and splashing can experience a kind of

1 Kaprow pursued the notion of un-art in the three part essay "The Education of the Un-Artist," to which the title of this text is a tribute. Developed between 1971-1974, it is perhaps Kaprow's most sustained critical project. See part 1, *Art News* 69, 10 (1971): 28-31; part 2, *Art News* 71, 3 (1972): 34-39; and part 3, *Art in America* 62, 1 (1974): 85-89; reprinted in Allan Kaprow and Jeff Kelley, *Essays on the Blurring of Art and Life* (Berkeley, Calif: Univ. of California Press, 2003) 97-109; 110-126; 130-147.

2 The terms *Superarchitettura* and Superarchitecture have variously been used by scholars to refer to a wide range of experimentation that took place in Italy between 1963 and 1973. These terms have been revitalized by Sylvia Lavin to denote the generation of architects Germano Celant (and later, Paola Navone, Bruno Orlandoni, Franco Raggi, Gianni Pettena, among others) grouped under the rubric Architettura Radicale. The term Superarchitecture was used before Lavin by Dominique Roulllard to designate a phenomenon broadly European in scope. See Sylvia Lavin, "Andy Architect™ — Or, a Funny Thing Happened on the way to the Disco," *Log* 15 (2009): 99-110; *Kissing Architecture* (Princeton, N.J: Princeton University Press, 2011) 51-62; and Dominique Rouillard, *Superarchitecture: le futur de l'architecture, 1950-1970* (Paris: Éditions de la Villette, 2004).

3 See Gianni Pettena, *L'anarchitetto: Portrait of the Artist As a Young Architect* (Rimini: Guaraldi, 1973). Critics have too readily aligned un-architecture with the architectural nihilism of the *superarchitetti* of Pettena's generation. Still, as will be discussed below, with Pettena such nihilism reaches another, more nounced stage, questioning the premises of *Superarchitettura*, spescifically its semiolgic bent.

> spatial extension... In the present case the "picture" has moved so far out that the canvas is no longer a reference point... [so that] art that tends to lose itself out of bounds, tends to fill our world with itself...[4]

Pollock's most striking works, like Kaprow's — his Happenings illuminate the point in a way no academic effort can match — make no bones about the occupation of the artist being an unbiased act, an action. Still, alongside Kaprow's elaborate performance pieces and his insistence on public participation, the 1958 reading prefigures a particular attention to questions of architecture and space. At the same time as Pollock's work becomes one activity among others, the boundaries framing the work as painting fade away, including those separating pictorial space and architectural spaces, and the specificity of one discipline with regards to the next.

Recent observers broached similar disciplinary dissolutions, from Hal Foster and his *Art-Architecture Complex* to Sylvia Lavin and David Joselit in their studies and didactic exhibitions.
These efforts have the merit of employing the facts relevant to architecture practice to account for the material fact and, even more, the theoretical premises of contemporary art.[5]
They offer a unique perspective on the current state of practice and surprisingly incisive discussions of its advances — say, as with Foster, in a close examination of Gehry Partners and the digital CATIA model used in the fabrication of Richard Serra's *Double Torqued Ellipse* series. Foster and others also struggle with questions regarding the division of disciplinary mediums. How does one come from the other? What makes the interrelations between visual art and architectural space increasingly available? What intimacies lie between art and architecture once they are confounded as media? Concepts such as "disciplinary complexes," "kissing mediums," and "nodal formats," betray the intensely satisfying exchange between fields, and a desire for more robust disciplinary safe-guards. Surprisingly, then, rather than the miracle of collaboration between the arts, what now emerges is another intimacy between the fields, one founded in their shared anxieties around terms such as "medium specificity," "formal autonomy," and "criticality." Seen in this light, Kaprow's ideology of un-art and Pettena's *anarchitettura* seem ready-made to diffuse exactly such anxieties.

4 Allan Kaprow, "The Legacy of Jackson Pollock," *Art News* 57, 6 (1958): 24-26, 55-57; reprinted in Allan Kaprow and Jeff Kelley 01-09.

5 The discussion of art-architecture complexes has dominated recent discussion of multimedia architecture and the problem it raises of medium specificity. See Hal Foster, *The Art-Architecture Complex* (London: Verso, 2011); Sylvia Lavin, *Kissing Architecture*, and Sylvia Lavin and Kimberli Meyer, the exhibition catalog *Everything Loose Will Land*, (Verlag für moderne Kunst Nürnberg, 2013); and David Joselit, *After Art*. (Princeton, N.J: Princeton University Press, 2013), discussions of which around architecture media were anticipated in *Feedback: Television against Democracy* (Cambridge, Mass: MIT Press, 2007); an important text linking Joslit's discussion of radical video art to the field is Kevin McMahon's "Guerillas, Architects, and Cable-TV: SCI-Arc's Videos in Context," Gannon, Todd, and Ewan Branda, *A Confederacy of Heretics* (Los Angeles, Calif: SCI-Arc Press in association with Getty Publications, 2013) 194-97.

As early as 1973, Pettena articulated the idea of un-architecture to bring into coherence a particularly intense period of production that stretched back to 1968, geographically dispersed between Florence, Palermo, Minneapolis, and Salt Lake City. In this period, Pettena was linked with a group artist and critics, including Smithson and the British art critic Lawrence Alloway, who were united by a single, special relationship with un-architecture. In the notes he kept during his tenure at the Minneapolis Institute of Art and Design and at the University of Utah between October 1970 and June 1972, Pettena described this relationship, citing the themes that entranced him some years earlier during his Florentine debut as a young artist while still an architecture student. "I first tried it with Bob," he writes of Smithson, "to make him say that he was an architect. And why? Because he is..." Bringing Alloway into the same conversation, in a passage later he continues to ask, "... but why should they be otherwise than what they are, architects?"[6]

Indeed, at the time of their meeting, Smithson had just turned his three year stint with the architecture firm Tippetts-Abbett-McCarthy-Stratton (working on proposals for the Dallas-Fort Worth Regional Airport) into *Spiral Jetty*. During his residency in Minneapolis, Pettena ran into Smithson by accident when out on a walk. The two had met earlier in Rome (during the fabrication of Smithson's *Asphalt Rundown*)[7] and Pettena offered Smithson a beer and conversation. Pettena instantly sympathized with Smithson's mixture of academic thinking and lack of reverence for academia. In spite of his experience in the field, Smithson treated architecture with an amused disdain. He talked about his projects for large scale monuments in Alaska and Canada, of his time with TAMS, and of Aerial Art, the scalability of building and mapping (Smithson was interested in boring). Then it was late, and Smithson had a long drive home.

The following day, straining to think through the coincidence, Pettena decided to take to the skies, repeatedly taking off and "land[ing] on the frozen lakes of Crosby. It was strange" he recalls, "Sunday morning inside that airplane in the cold over the city, *and it came to me to use ice* — the easiest thing as usual. Cold and heat, fire and water. As usual there was a script to prepare and then everything would be smooth as ever. I was trying but it was difficult to do these things with isolated houses. Twenty-two permits required. The school was easier."[8] Thus were born the monuments of *Ice House I* and *II*.

6 Pettena, *L'anarchitetto* 22.

7 Cf. in this publication, "Dialogues: Gianni Pettena and Emanuele Piccardo," 109-118.

8 Pettena, *L'anarchitetto* 47. My Italics.

9 On the events of the *Masaccio*, see UFO, "Urboeffimeri avvenenti scala 1/1," *Marcatré* 41-42 (1968): 76-82; Tommaso Trini, "Masaccio a UFO," *Domus* 466: 55-56; and my "Superurbeffimero n. 7: Umberto Eco's Semiologia and the Architectural Rituals of the UFO," *California Italian Studies* 2, 2 (2011).

10 Trini 56. Unless stated otherwise, all translations are my own.

11 *Urboeffemero* is a portmanteau word combining "urban" and "ephemera". The definition of the *urboeffimeri* as architectural Happenings is given in the group's self-published pamphlet, titled "UFO.: HAPPENING ! INTENSA ECCITAZIONE PLASTICO – TATTILE! UFO. UFFF...FFFF." The pamphlet was distributed by the UFO on June 24, 1968, the night of the performance at Valdarno.

12 UFO 76.

Pettena's first came to his own with an intervention conceived for the city of San Giovanni Valdarno at the sixth *premio di pittura Masaccio* of June 1968.[9] Notably, the event's date coincided with the procession for the city's patron saint, and the incident escalated into a public riot and later led to an inquiry by the *magistratura* into suspicions of blasphemy. The controversy surrounding the *Masaccio* started earlier however, in response to Pettena's transformation of the façade of Palazzo d'Arnolfo. Pettena re-dressed the building's double loggia — which run along the front and rear of the building — with a simple pattern of silver strips of aluminum cooking foil. As Tommaso Trini observed at the time, this straightforward, low-tech economy saw the intelligent and ironic reversal of architectural "conventions: the old palace — Renaissance monument — became a compact sign, the architectural volume was reduced to the flatness of the façade,... [and] the container of the exhibition and its function became, in fact, themselves the object of visual experience."[10] Moreover, the alien image of the Commune's tower that resulted against the luminescence of Pettena's aluminum fields — with Palazzo d'Arnolfo undone by intermittent gapping voids — became itself the protagonist in the Happening set for the occasion by UFO, the other Superarchitecture group to participate in the *Masaccio*. The program for the Happening, the *Urboeffimero*,[11] begins:

Start...

Start...

Barnard...

Start

An unidentified object gets jammed right on the roof of the Valdarnese town hall.... The great alchemist finds his conventional habitat in this preexisting high ground and there he takes shelter. From his *pied-à-tour* the great alchemist organizes the virgins at the *pied-à-toit* and the technicians *pied-à-terre.*"[12]

In print, at least, Pettena and UFO shared an interest in questions of architecture and language and the manipulation of the architectural sign. The possibility of applying linguistics to architecture came to the Florentine *superarchitetti* chiefly through art critic Gillo Dorfles, who had been appointed professor of "Decorazione" in 1959 — succeeded by Umberto Eco between 1966 and 1969. Dorfles' and Eco's positions varied, but only within certain parameters. While Eco's theory of visual communication, with its open structures of doubly-laid signification patterns, was opposed to Dorfles' semantic and psychological assumptions, both were engrossed in a semiotic rethinking of architecture. Intrinsically, they were intent on decoding and reconfiguring architecture's constituent, primary elements — whether, as with Dorfles, towards the assemblage of a coherent, rationalist discourse within a clear referential system, or, as with Eco, towards the complete suspension of the architectural signified and the mobilization of the same system within a visual, iconic continuum.

In San Giovanni Valdarno, it was Eco's position that prevailed. Closer to Eco, UFO pursued the manipulation of local icons: the fourteenth century Palazzo d'Arnolfo, the great transverse urban corridor of Piazza Cavour, the monument for Garibaldi, and the Marzocco. And yet UFO's Happening also went further, forcing on the public a different set of iconic codes and urging it to reinterpret and decode these monuments through their active reuse. The group brought to fruition the iconic continuum theorized by Eco with explicit semiologic devices ("secret weapon connotation") and related themes, including the popular novel (James Bond) and advertising. In Pettena's transformation of Palazzo d'Arnolfo, rather than a play on local iconicity, the basic operation was of the effect of light on metal. Indeed, rather than semiotic, the work turned on the material and affective residues that underlie all symbolic/ semiotic operations when connected to the deeper history of architecture, primarily that of the architectural surface. This was done by rethinking the lighting features originally intended by the Valdarnese Commune as to accentuate the palazzo's deep, doubly-laid loggias. Caught by Pettena's aluminum foils, light would now come in not so much from below as from the side, following the oblique direction of metal sheeting.[13]

On the evidence of Pettena's text of 1979, the last point was a not-unfriendly critique of the language-like manipulations of architecture.[14] The study's title *Effimero urbano e città* is as much a

13 Alongside this materiality of effect, Pettena's oblique pattern converses with the hard-edged, polychromatic patterns of zigzags and wavy strips that ornate the *superarchitetture* of Archizoom and Superstudio, under the influence of the Pistoiese circle of Pop artists closer to Adolfo Natalini. This architecture-art complex with Pop Art motives appear also throughout the thesis projects of the young *superarchitetti*, for example in Natalini's and Massimo Morozzi's thesis — respectively Palazzo dell'Arte di Firenze and Centro Culturale dentro il Castello dell'Imperatore a Prato — while the latter also includes the reproduction of another American Pop Art icon: James Rosenquist's *F-111* (1965). See the thorough discussion in Roberto Gargiani, *Archizoom Associati, 1966-1974: Dall'onda Pop Alla Superficie Neutra* (Milan: Electa, 2007) 18-28.

14 In this little known rebuttal to Emil Kaufman — and the architectural narrative of Modernism's neoclassical origins — Pettena posits the great festivals of 1893 Paris as the true architectural harbingers of the Revolution. See Emil Kaufmann's canonical "Three Revolutionary Architects: Boullée, Ledoux, and Lequeu," *Philadelphia* (American Philosophical Society: 1952); and Gianni Pettena, *Effimero urbano e città: le feste della parigi rivoluzionaria* (Venezia: Marsilio, 1979).

nod to the UFO group and their Happenings of 1968, the *urboeffimeri*, as it is a critique of these Happenings' semiotic premise. The text presents an analysis of the essentially ephemeral and "undurable architectures" of the great festivals of 1893 Paris, and a thesis about their essential qualities, the key point being their imperviousness to the exploitation of "superfluous messages and their deviations."[15]

In the year of the *Masaccio*, Pettena exploited this good-natured and coherent critique of the field's semiotic turn to stunning effect. The tripartite performance *Carabinieri*, *Milite Ignoto*, and *Grazia & Giustizia* (beginning in Novara, with a stop in Ferrara, and terminating in Palermo)[16] carried this position to its logical conclusion. Each segment of the performance saw the further de-structuring of the process of architectural signification. Pettena's ironic *mise-en-scène* of the architectural signified was performed with thirty-nine, 220 cm high cardboard walls, shaped as letters, and grouped to spell out each segment's title. Lasting between one day to a week—the letters quickly decayed in the summer rains in Novara and Ferrara. In Palermo, the letters for *Grazia & Giustizia were carried* in a mock-funerary procession across town, down to the historic port. Again, Pettena's work precipitated from the material effect of the letters' self-obsolescence, rather than from semiotic critique. As the students began to march, the unwieldy and oversized cardboard signs began to deteriorate. The photo taken at Palermo's docks (just minutes before the letters' final disposal) somewhat approximates the effect, showing the defaced G of GIUSTIZIA, standing out among the general wreck of cardboard typography, awkwardly bowed, draped over a nearby railing. Other questions arise here: disengagement from Modernist concerns with the industrially precise detail, for example, and the attendant possibilities of "awkward positions" and "postures."[17] Seen in this light, rather than simply de-structured, Pettena's cardboard typography approximates figures without syntax and anticipates, for better or worse, the mutable menagerie of co-dependent, weak-at-the-knees architectures of the present.

None of this makes Pettena's un-architecture any less serious, of course, but the fact remains that the power of his work turns on an architectural intuition about matter. The specific focus, in the *House* series and beyond, concerns surface envelopes. Indeed, one of the novel aspects here is the insistence on the architectural surface — an experiment with architecture's exteriority and its susceptibility

15 Pettena, *Effimero* 10.

16 Respectively performed at Palazzo Comunale, Novara, Palazzo dei Diamanti, Ferrara, and at the VI Festival di Musica d'Avanguardia, Palermo.

17 See, for instance, Andrew Zago's recent "Awkward Position," *Perspecta* 42 (2013): 209-22; and Jeffrey Kipnis and Stephen Turk, *Figure Ground Game, An Architecturalists Show*, SCI-Arc Gallery, 17 January – 2 March 2014.

to the environment (humidity, rain, but also the sounds and the vitality and verve of a passing procession). With this last point, exteriority itself became an effect of the site as much as a medium towards its realization and so the vital key in this relationship.
In the years that followed groups and architects as diverse as SITE, Hans Hollein, Wolf Prix, and Frank Gehry would further develop the notion of the entropic envelope. By the mid-Nineties the envelope's affectivity — rather than its historical context, its symbolic referent, or even its efficiency — became viable models of architectural with Rudy Ricciotti and Herzog & de Meuron. The material/affective instinct, which Pettena exercised in the 1968 performances, is similarly active in the American monuments of the early 1970s: *Ice House I* and *II*.

The *House* series does with ruthless economy of means what most architects today do through excess of processes and systems. Staged in Minneapolis in an abandoned school and in a nondescript suburban house, Pettena poured water onto the mold works he had created with his students around the buildings' perimeter walls. Curing during the winter night to a coat of ice, the *Houses* resonated with their conceptual predecessor *Fluids*, the mass Happening staged in 1967 as part of the Kaprow's large scale retrospective at the Pasadena Art Museum. *Fluids* and the intimate corollary of its fifteen structures to architecture has been widely discussed by Philip Ursprung and, earlier, Jack Burnham and Richard Kostelanetz. Kaprow of course, insisted on the analog of architecture and its potential for his art as early as 1958, when reading Pollock's anti-painterly method as an architectural expansion of the field. This new purview was immediately experimented in *Environment* the same year. However, by the end of the Sixties, Kaprow grew increasingly concerned with the phenomenological problem of site. Political hostility marred the terrain, and architecture, which was so integrated with the early Environments and Happenings, itself became a site for contention. In *Fluids* this new attitude was emphasized by Kaprow's staging of key operations of the multipart Happening within "the twilight zone of indifferent architecture" for the disenfranchised.[18] These site included three Pasadena lots, one just south of a McDonald's restaurant, the others under two Colorado Street bridges; the fourth a foothold in Watts, the South Los Angeles neighborhood notorious for the 1965 riots.[19] This sensibility would turn progressively more aggressive in *Transfer* (*A Happening for Christo*, 1968), *Overtime* (*For Walter De Maria*, 1968; parts of which are currently reproduced

18 Allan Kaprow, conversation with Philip Ursprung, 1997, reproduced in *Allan Kaprow, Robert Smithson*: 110.

19 See reproduction of *Fluids*' program in this publication, 84.

at LACE), and *Sweet Wall* (1970), the latter a solid brick wall, erected and then dismantled adjacent to the Berlin Wall.[20] Against Kaprow's political critique of the built environment — made explicit in the repetitive, labor intense stacking and assembling of more than 400,000 pounds of ice —[21] Pettena's *Houses* present a distinctly elegant engagement with building possibilities and means. In general, *Ice House I* offers a more coherent and consistently worked-out argument than the later project. Pettena seems to have experienced real difficulty at the time, but also real advances, within the economy of in-situ concrete casting. Replacing concrete with ice, *Ice House I's* underlying four-story existing school — marked by clear datum planes confirmed by the fenestration and limestone — are transformed and given a milky patina. The determining factors are the extreme temperatures of the Minnesota winter plus the fire hydrants located around the perimeter of the school. Surrounding the structure, these *objets trouvés* were interconnected via variedly laid casting tubes. Providing a constant, homogenous pour, Pettena strategically placed the casting tubs at the extremities of the building, forming a new, superior datum plane. The choice to overlay a new datum plane over and above the exiting structure was confirmed a day later, when the perimeter molding was removed. The smoothly compounded ice created an experience of formal/visual undecidability — a consistently present frustration of datum planes and fenestration rhythms. Readings of the existing, underlying structure became strained and ambiguous. So while the existing structure's recessed symmetries and center-to-edge conditions persisted, the window/architrave grid was erased and frustrated, resulting in a new, solid-state architecture of ice. For *Ice House II* there was a further uncertainty concerning the status of "house." Unlike its predecessor, which was set in an open park, *Ice House II* was located within a row of anonymous, two-story suburban homes. The viewer/participant would continually readjust, moving between the appropriate condition of the gabbled-roof home and Pettena's abstracted cubic prism of the same scale and disposition.

By the time Pettena returned to Florence, after his New York solo exhibit at the John Weber Gallery in 1972,[22] the phenomenon of Superarchitecture was already known as Radical Architecture (after critic Germano Celant) and was pretty much over. Pettena appeared in the cabal's closing festivities, those at the foundation of the short-lived Global Tools consortium in Milan, 1973, but only under the dual roles of outsider "spectator" and

20 All the above architecturally scaled Happenings were varied permutations of Kaprow's new understanding of architecture as the unavoidable, if "amplifiable … defining mechanism" of the gallery space. Such repositioning was accompanied, in turn, by a plea to others to break through the "fences [that the architectural frame builds] around … human acts and thoughts." See Allan Kaprow, "The Shape of the Art-Environment: How Anti-Form Is 'Anti-Form'?," *Artforum* 6, 10 (Summer 1968): 33; reprinted in Jeff Kelley, *Essays on the Blurring of Art and Life* (Berkeley, Calif: Univ. of California Press, 2003) 92.

21 Less discussed than Kaprow's struggles with the domineering space of architecture are the dynamics implicit to Kaprow's built productions: the mobilization, engineering, as well as the schedule, permitting, and human labors entailed by specialized building labors. The last fact, that of labor, would find its clearest voice in Alloway's note of the 1970s expansions of the art field: "[w]hen he came to operate in enlarged dimensions, the conditions of...[the] work changed drastically. He found himself out of the studio and no longer dependent on middle agents for the handling of his work...he had to deal directly with contractors, engineers, realtors, executives, and civic officials, ... Accompanying this expansion of operations the view he takes of galleries and museums has hardened." The case, made in and around the same time as Pettena's *Houses*, of Smithson's turn to architectural scaled work (and away from Minimalism), might have been equally applied to the Kaprow of *Fluids*. See Lawrence Alloway, "Robert Smithson's Development" *Artforum* 11, 3 (November 1972) 52-61.

22 See Joseph Masheck, "Gianni Pettena, Italian artist," *Artforum* 10, 10 (June 1972) 60-63.

"*spia*."[23] Not surprisingly, his affinities remained closer to Smithson and to the latter's elegant sidestepping of media boundaries and conventions. "Bob," he reasoned, was "evading the question of architecture with a lot of eloquence. Such statements and readings both he and Lawrence [Alloway] avoid. They avoid talking about architecture, it is a much too contaminated terrain, burdened with too much thinking and mindedness."[24] Pettena's — and Smithson's — architecture-art complex, the engagement with matter and affect, as well as the lucid critique of the "mindedness" of architectural meaning would not survive Charles Jenks and George Baird, Postmodern architecture, American "criticality" and the respective "autonomies" of Italian and American architecture. Pettena's cardboard structures and his *Houses*, however, survive, and the novel sensibilities they provoked at the time of their making remain relevant as ever.

23 "I am and I'm not, I'm here and I'm not, I'm the spy so I'm here than, actor and spectator, always the spy, that is I don't belong, but I pretend to, so to see what happens, then I run to report..." Pettena, *L'anarchitetto* 57.

24 Pettena, *L'anarchitetto* 22.

Λ 49
Allan Kaprow
and Unidentified
Record II
1968
The Getty Research Institute
Los Angeles

Dialogues: Gianni Pettena and Robert Smithson

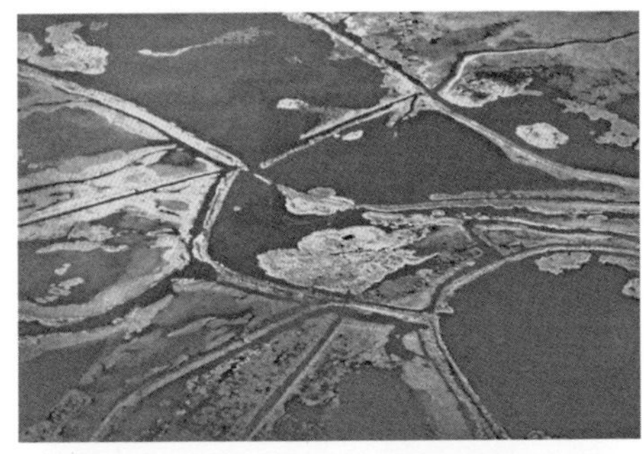

< 52 – 58
Gianni Pettena
About non conscious architecture
USA, 1972-1973
Gianni Pettena Archive
Fiesole

∧ 59
Tom Kass
Lawrence Alloway
Robert Smithson
Gianni Pettena
Spiral Jetty
Salt Lake City, 1972
Gianni Pettena Archive
Fiesole

< 60 ∧ 61
Robert Smithson
Asphalt Rundown
Rome, Via Laurentina, 1969
photographs by
Claudio Abate

< 62 Λ 63 > 64 – 65
Robert Smithson
Asphalt Rundown
Rome, Via Laurentina, 1969
photographs by
Claudio Abate

> 66 – 67
Gianni Pettena
Tumbleweeds catcher
Installation, Pine boards
and tumbleweeds
Salt Lake City, USA, 1972
Gianni Pettena Archive
Fiesole

> 68 – 69
Gianni Pettena
Clay house
during performance
Salt Lake City, USA, 1972
Gianni Pettena Archive
Fiesole

803

A conversation
in Salt Lake City
25 Jan. 1972

From: *Domus* 516 (1972)

RS

We could start out with the idea that I had at the beginning of the lecture (University of Utah, Jan. 24, 1972) about recycling quarries, disused mining areas and that sort of things in terms of art. Working in industrial areas that are no longer used – disused areas. That's the thing that I'm interested in. Sonsbeek in Holland indicated a direction away from the centralized museum into something more social, and less esthetic. I would say mainly in Europe one would have to work in a quarry or in a mining area, because everything is so cultivated in terms of the Church or aristocracy. The rest is all middle-class versions of that kind of cultivation.

GP

I kind of agree about that, thinking about the distinction you made between here and Europe. That's essential. Here, let's say you've got a lot of land and there they don't. That's the difference.
I also agree on your choice of sites. I think I understand why you prefer dismissed areas rather than untouched areas.
But the fact is that for me those areas are still too natural.
That is to say that, for me, natural, dismissed or untouched areas are really the same thing. All of them are natural and not exactly the place for a work of mine. I have no right to touch a natural area and an old disused mine it's a place that nature recycled according to its standards, thus subtracting it to me.

RS

I think you have to find a site that is free of scenic meaning. Scenery has too many built-in meanings that relate to stagey isolated views. I prefer views that are expansive, that include everything...

GP

I'm thinking that perhaps you are able to do something in a town in Europe while you are not able to do something in a town here.

RS

Well, I can't really work in towns. I have to work in the outskirts or in the fringe areas, in the backwaters. The real estate too, in the towns, too, is too expensive. So that it's a practical, actually, to go out to wasteland areas whether they're natural or manmade and reconvert those into situations. The Salt Lake piece is right near a disused oil drilling operation and the whole northern part of the lake is completely useless. I'm interested in bringing a landscape with low profile up, rather than bringing one with high profile down. The macro aggression that goes into certain _______earthworks_______ doesn't interest me.

GP

There's no need to choose, then, a nice landscape.

RS

Beauty spots, they call them. Nature with class.

GP

That's exactly what some groups of architects are doing.
They are doing photo-montage (not real) proposals on conceptual architecture and they have often to choose very beautiful or very famous landscapes, postcards landscapes, in a way which will support their idea. The fundamental position of putting a light under a painting to light it.

RS

Or put a balloon tent structure on a landscape that's already cultivated. I think that should be avoided. I'm not interested in that kind of thing... World's Fair kind of architecture. It suggest the future that will never come...
I'm more interested right now in things that are sort of sprawling and imbedded in the landscape rather than putting an object on the landscape.

GP

I'm not avoiding anything which is in the landscape, but in an urban landscape. Because for me it's the only place, as you were saying about Sonsbeek, where you can make something more social and less esthetic.

RS

Well, New York itself is natural like the Grand Canyon. We have to develop a different sense of nature; we have to develop a dialectic of nature that includes man... A kind of "virgin", beauty was established in the early days of this country and most people who don't look too hard tend to see the world through postcards and calendars so that affects their idea of what they think nature should be rather than what it is.

GP

I remember once I was with a German friend of mine and we were looking at a beautiful landscape near the University. There was a helicopter in the sky, far and still like a black point but one could notice it. My friend asked what it was and I answered him that it was a printing mistake...

RS

I like landscapes that suggest prehistory. As an artist it is sort of interesting to take on the persona of a geologic agent where man actually becomes part of that process rather than overcoming it... rather than overcoming the natural processes of challenging the situation. You just go along with it, and there can be a kind of building that takes place this way...
I did an article once, on Passaic, New Jersey, a kind of rotting industrial town where they were building a highway along the river. It was somewhat devastated. In a way, this article that I wrote on Passaic could be conceived of as a kind of appendix to William Carlos William's poem "Patterson".
It comes out of that kind of New Jersey ambiance where everything is chewed up. New Jersey like a kind of destroyed California, a derelict California.

GP

Another work I did was exactly in a place where they were building a highway. You know, sometimes for me it is difficult to make that kind of observations because you really have to find a place that doesn't work any more like a town but still has to look like a town. Or you can use the town while it is still working but then there are always many difficulties. You really can't...

RS

You really can't. There's a word called entropy. These are kind of like entropic situations that hold themselves together. It's like the *Spiral Jetty* is physical enough to be able to withstand all these climate changes, yet it's intimately involved with those climate changes and natural disturbances.That's why I'm not really interested in conceptual art because that seems to avoid physical mass. You're left mainly with an idea. Somehow to have something physical that generates ideas is more interesting to me than just an idea that might generate something physical.

GP

I think the main tension of something so called conceptual can be really a kind of old way to think about physicality.

RS

It's very idealistic. It's basically a kind of reductionism. A lot of it verges on a cultism and pseudoconscience and that sort of thing. Conceptual art is a kind of reduced object down to a notion of ideas that leads to idealism. An idealism is a kind of spiritualism and that never seems to work out.

GP

I wouldn't be so drastic. I'm only thinking that what has been said and done speaking about language, was very important and has been useful to several people. I think that only after what Art & Language etc, asserted, one can go back to a certain physicality after learning the lesson. There's no longer need of being afraid to do something physical but what you do must show that you learnt that lesson. That physicality doesn't bother you because you control it and it is simply a physical support to the concepts you communicate.

RS

It's interesting too, in looking at the slides of ruins there's always a sense of highly developed structures in the process of disintegration. You could go and look for the great temple and it's in ruins, but you rarely go looking for the factory or highway that's in ruins. Lévi Strauss suggested that they change the word anthropology to entropology, meaning highly developed structures in a state of disintegration. I think that's part of the attraction of people going to visit obsolete civilizations. They get a gratification from the collapse of these things. The same experience can be felt in suburban architecture, in what they call the "slurbs".

GP

I feel the same way about suburban architecture and this is generally the area where I like to work.

RS

It could apply to anything actually. There is no taste differential actually.

GP

Once, in Italy, some people (artists) were invited to do something as an intervention on a town. We had all the town. We could work in every part of the town, but strangely enough everybody chose the main square.

RS

They all run towards the center because that's the more secure place.

GP

Every town, downtown, has nice, clean rich buildings which are an expression of power and make you feel secure.
But in the meantime you have to remember that this is generally a visualization of power. And the suburbs are exactly the contrary.
At that time. In 1969, I got mad thinking about this kind of choice that everyone was making. Choosing the space of power only because it was nice and clean. In this way, all the town was seen and interpreted even if correctly and honestly only through the main square, which was used like a simple gallery space...

RS

You put a clothesline into the square?

GP

I put some clotheslines into the square to rebuild a deemphatization.

RS

So that's sort of like bringing the fringes into the main square.

GP

This was very intentional.

RS

The clotheslines are an interesting thing to bring into the main plaza.

GP

Yes, I did It this way intentionally to correct this kind of emphatization. I think this was me only chance anyone ever had to put a clothesline in a main square. And looking at the catatogue of this show, I would say it really worked out. In fact every work or intervention has these clotheslines In the background.

RS

The notions of centrality give people a security and certainty because it's also a place where most people gather. But they tend to forget the fringes. I have a dialectic between the center and the outer circumferences. You realty can't get rid of this notion of centrality nor can you get rid of the fringes and they both sort of feed on each other. It's kind of Interesting to bring the fringes into the centrality and the centrality out to the fringes. I developed that somewhat with the non-sites where I would go out to a fringe area and send back the raw material to New York City, which is a kind of center... a big sprawling nightmare center, but it's still there. Then that goes into the gallerv and the non-site functions as a map that tells you where the fringes are. it's rare trat anybody will visit these fringes, but it's interesting to know about them.

GP

You always show the places from which you are coming,

.

.

.

.

.

.

.

.

.

.

if you are sincere.

Dialogues: Gianni Pettena and Allan Kaprow

< 78 Λ 79
Gianni Pettena
Ice House I
Installation, water and rubber hoses
Minneapolis, USA, 1971
Gianni Pettena Archive
Fiesole

> 80 – 81
Gianni Pettena
Ice House II
Installation, water and rubber hoses
Gianni Pettena Archive
Fiesole

> 82 – 83
Allan Kaprow
Fluids, Performance
Pasadena, USA, 1967
photograph by
Julian Wasser
The Getty Research Institute
Los Angeles

McCLELLAN

Six models!

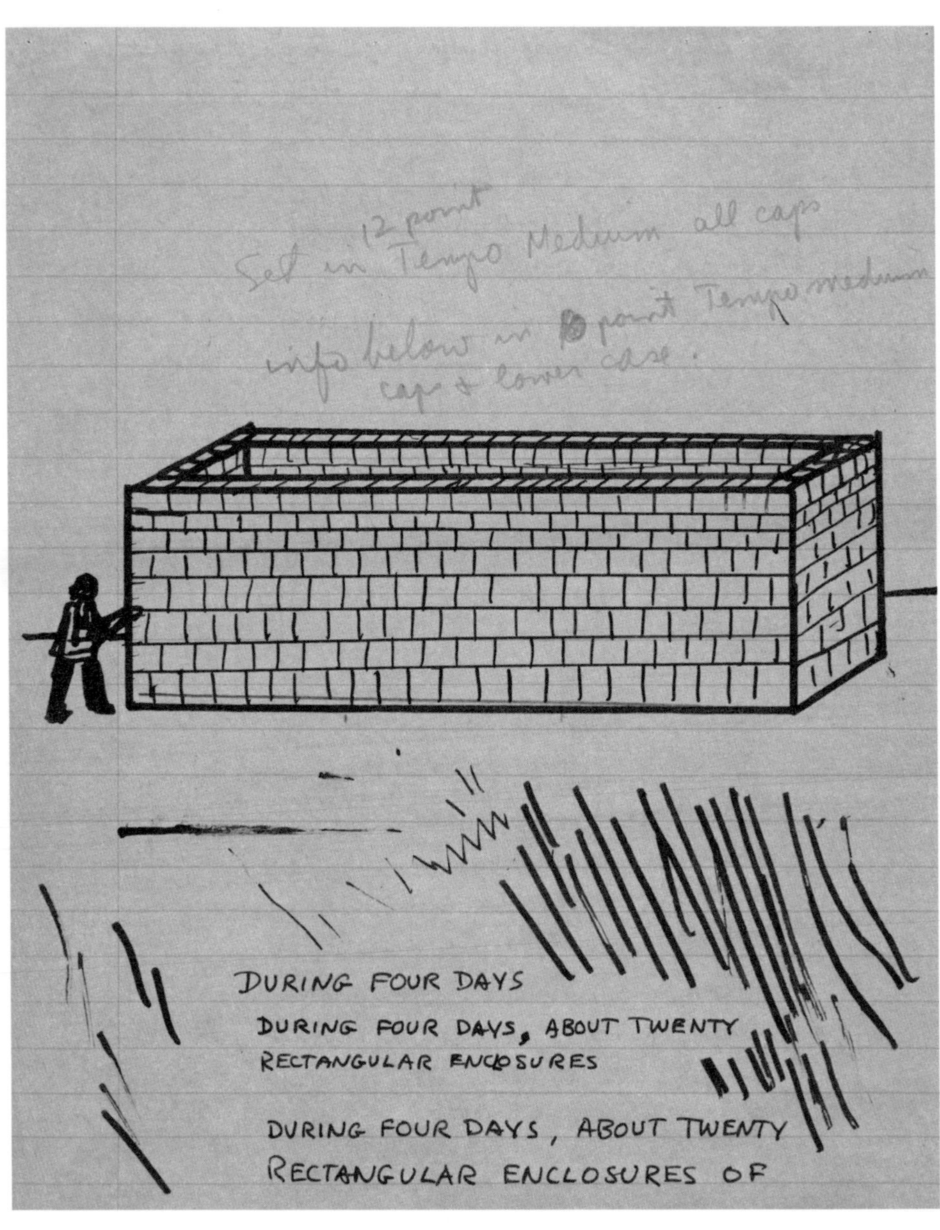

Λ 84
Allan Kaprow
Fluids
Sketch for poster/score,
Happening sponsored by
Pasadena Art Museum, 1967
The Getty Research Institute
Los Angeles

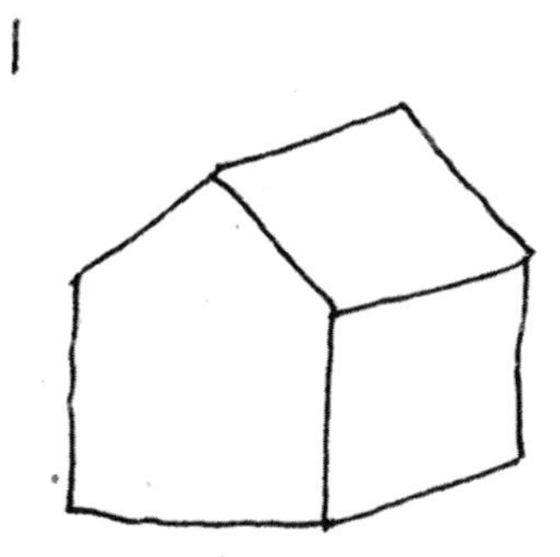

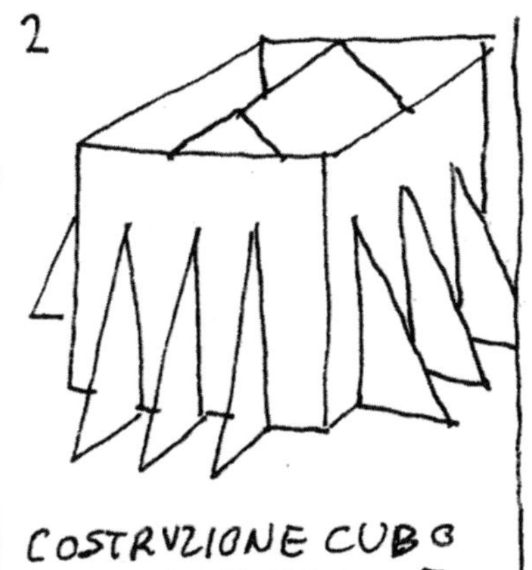

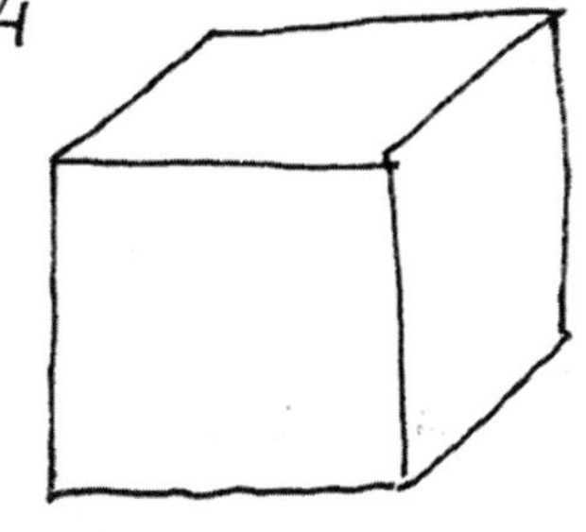

Λ 85
Gianni Pettena
Sketch for Ice House II
water and rubber hoses
Gianni Pettena Archive
Fiesole

> 86 – 87
Allan Kaprow
Fluids
1967
photograph by
Bruce Breland
The Getty Research Institute
Los Angeles

< 88 ∧ 89
Allan Kaprow
Record II
1968
The Getty Research Institute
Los Angeles

> 90 – 91
Gianni Pettena
Wearable chairs
Performance
Minneapolis, USA, 1971
Gianni Pettena Archive
Fiesole

NICOLLET

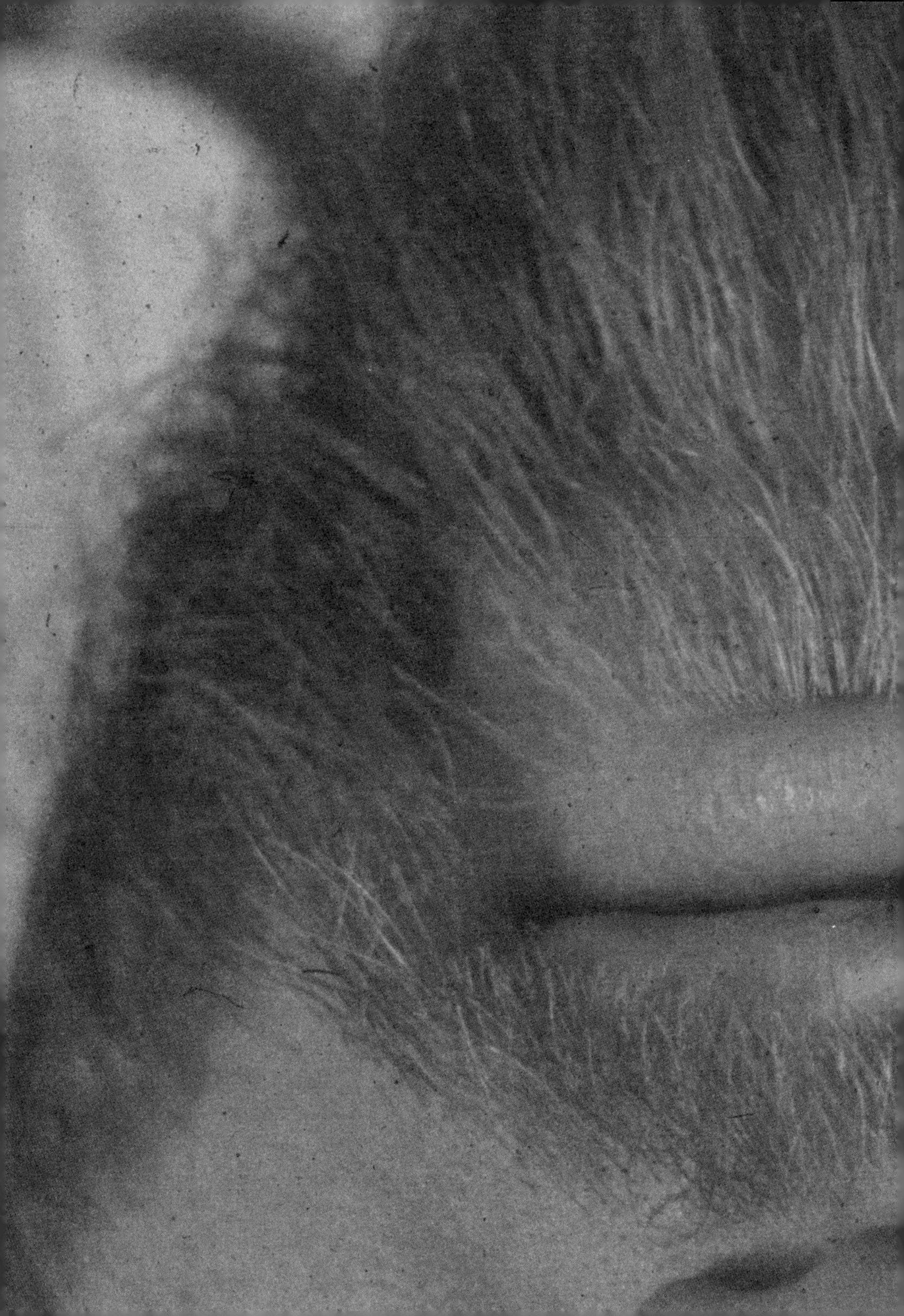

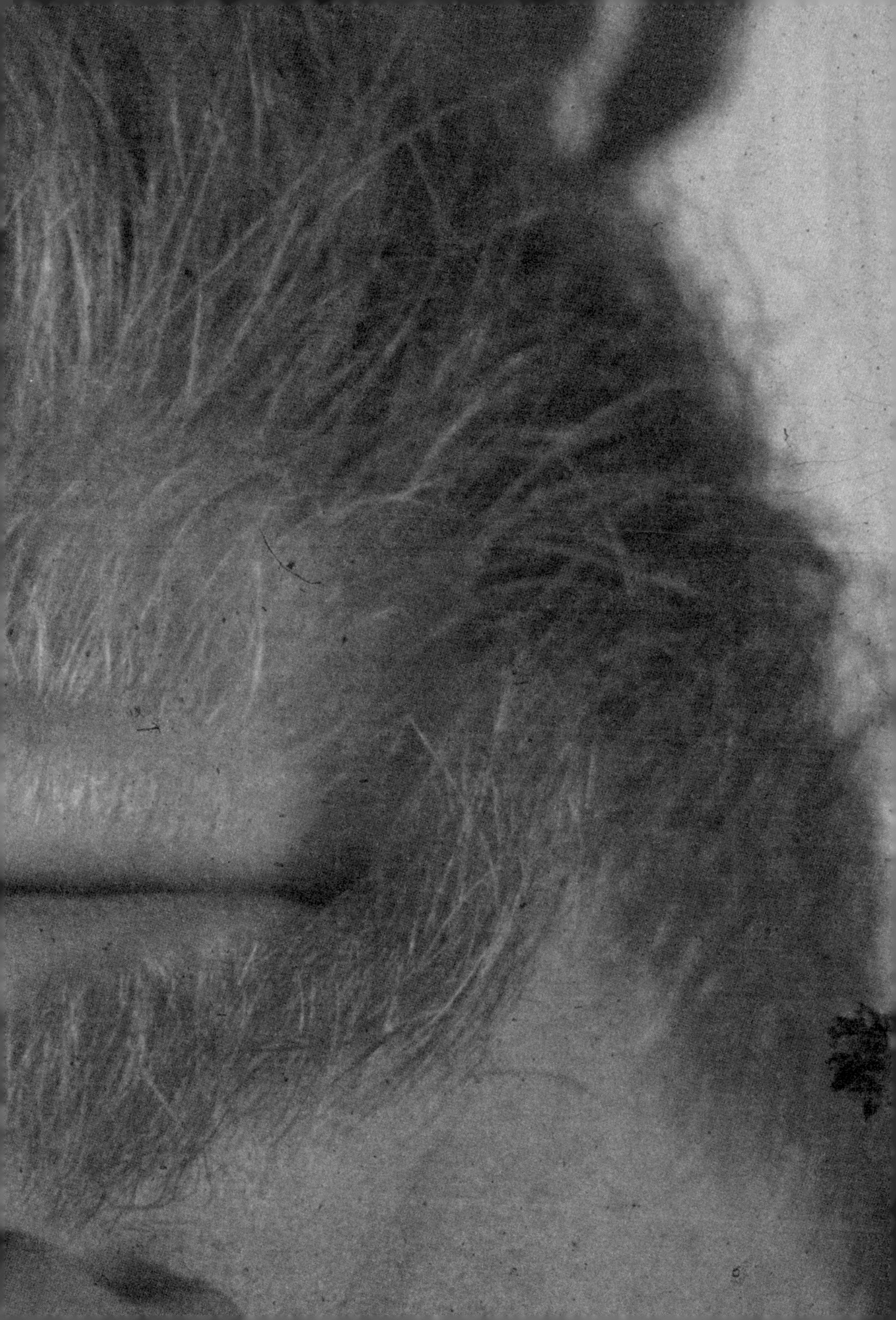

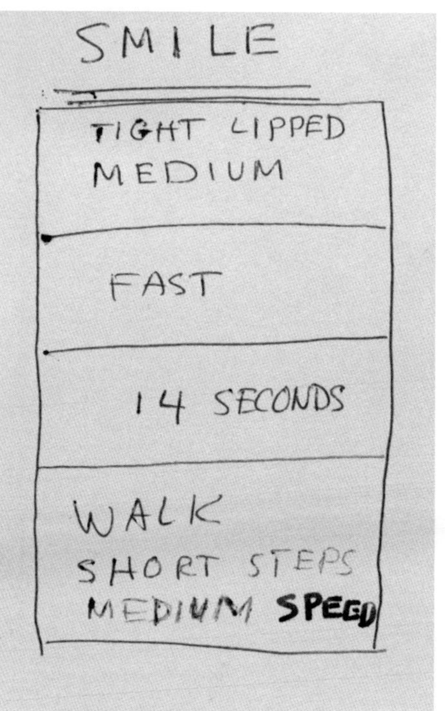

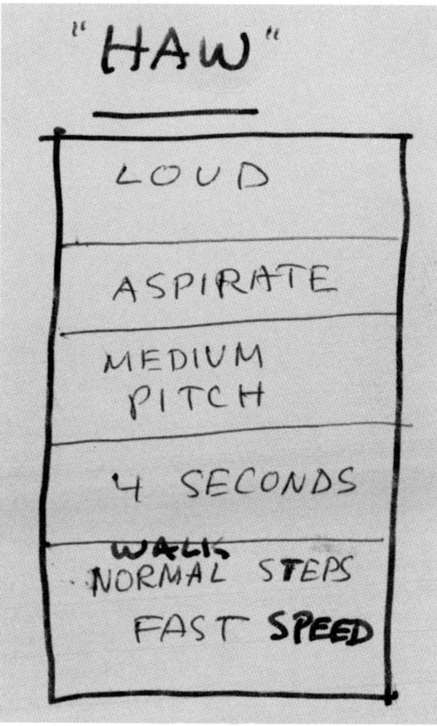

< 92 – 93
Allan Kaprow
18 Happenings in 6 parts: Smile
Happening
Reuben Gallery, New York
1959
The Getty Research Institute
Los Angeles

Λ 94
Allan Kaprow,
18 Happenings in 6 parts: audience instructions Smile and How
Happening
Reuben Gallery, New York
1959
The Getty Research Institute
Los Angeles

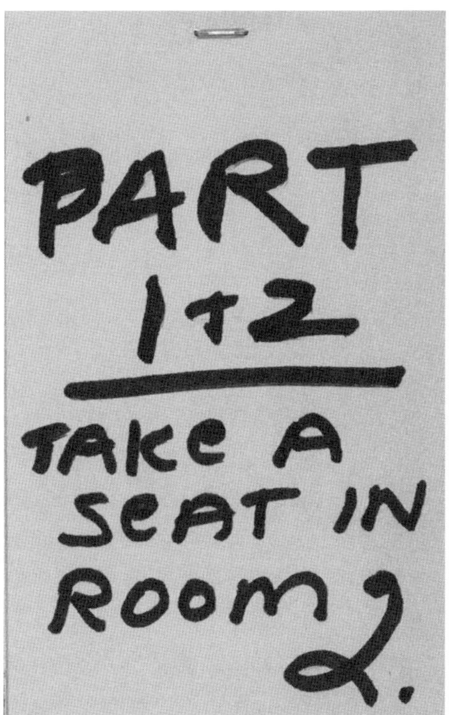

Λ 95
Allan Kaprow,
18 Happenings in 6 parts:
Audience instructions
Reuben Gallery, New York
1959
The Getty Research Institute
Los Angeles

REUBEN GALLERY

61 Fourth Avenue, New York City

Dear Sir:

Eighteen happenings will take place on October 2, 3, 4 and 9, 10, 11 at 8:30 P.M.

You are invited to collaborate with the artist, Mr. Allan Kaprow, in making these events take place. You are invited to collaborate in two ways:

First: Your presence at the Reuben Gallery is respectfully requested. As one of seventy-five persons present, you will become a part of the happenings; you will simultaneously experience them. To quote from Mr. Kaprow:

> In this different art, the artist takes off from life. Think of a buying spree at Macy's; how to grow geraniums in New York. Do not look for paintings, sculpture, the dance, or music. The artist disclaims any intention to provide them. He does believe that he provides some engaging situations...

For the record, Allan Kaprow's past activities include thirteen one-man exhibitions -- the last four related to this present work. He was a co-founder of the Hansa Gallery; showed at the Boston Arts Festival; the Jewish Museum's "New York School, Second Generation"; was chosen with a color reproduction for Art in America's "New Talent Quarterly"; will have two works reproduced in a forthcoming article in "La Revue Moderne des Arts et de Vie"; and was part of the American section of this past season's Carnegie International at Pittsburgh.

The present event is created in a medium which Mr. Kaprow finds refreshing to leave untitled.

You -- the audience -- will sit in numbered seats...but only the artist may reveal his intent at the proper place and time. Meantime, lights, lumber, paint, performers... all of these bring us to the second way in which you are invited to collaborate if you wish.

Second: Work has already begun; the summer-closed gallery is a flourish of activity. The assumption is that the adventuresome will be generous. Succinctly, money is needed. Yours. May we have your contribution now, early, when it will do the most good?

Sincerely,

Anita Reuben Berman

Reuben-Kaprow Associates

P.S. An unrevised "script", or abstract of the projected happenings was recently published in the Rutgers "Anthologist". If you would like a reprint, please write to Mr. Allan Kaprow c/o Reuben Gallery, 61 Fourth Avenue, New York City.

Λ 96
Allan Kaprow
18 Happenings in 6 parts
Invitation
Reuben Gallery, New York
1959
The Getty Research Institute
Los Angeles

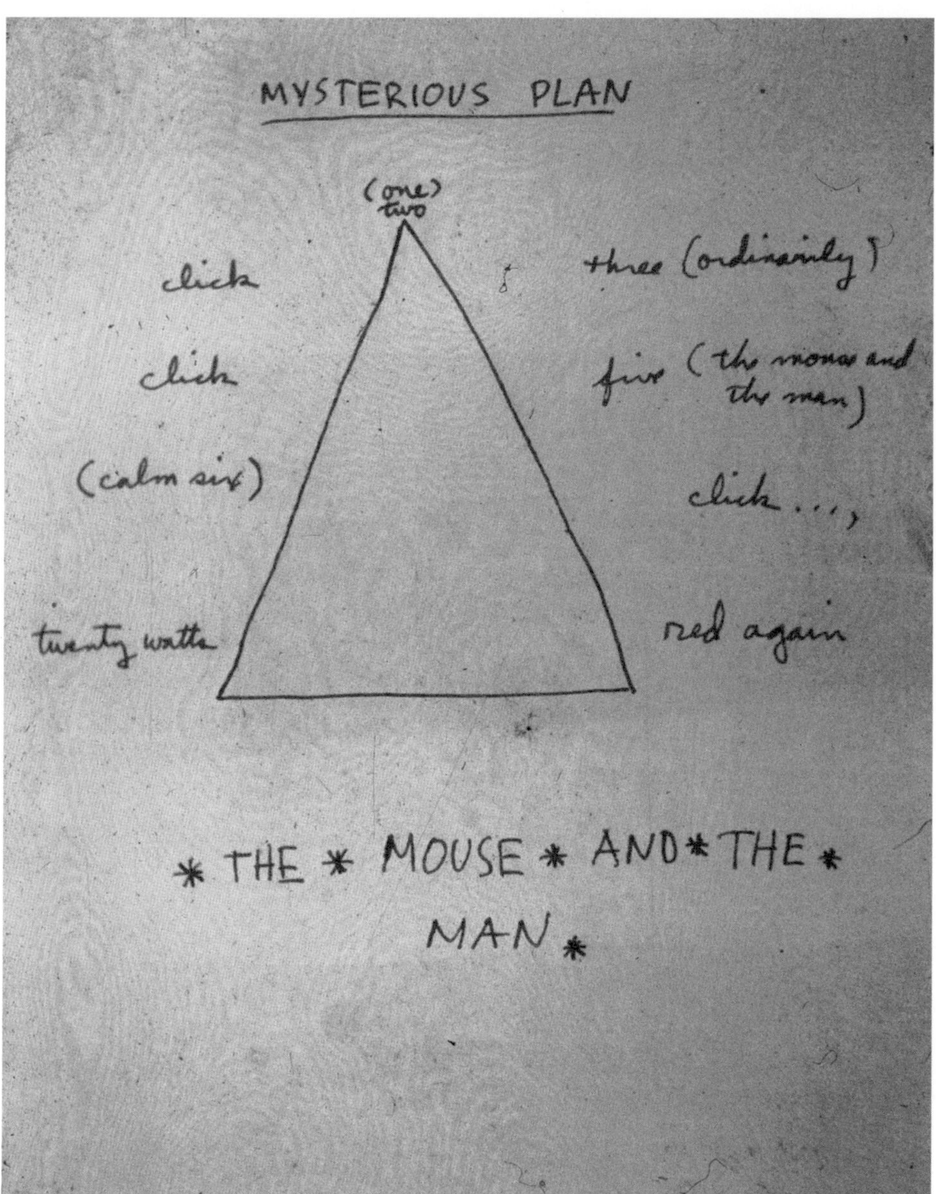

Λ 97
Allan Kaprow
18 Happenings in 6 parts
slideshow in room 3
Reuben Gallery, New York
1959
The Getty Research Institute
Los Angeles

Dialogues: Gianni Pettena and Gordon Matta-Clark

Λ 100
Gianni Pettena
Ice House II
Minneapolis, USA, 1971
Gianni Pettena Archive
Fiesole

Λ 101
Gordon Matta-Clark
A W-Hole House
Roof top atrium
Genoa, Galleria Forma, 1973
Camec, Cozzani collection
La Spezia

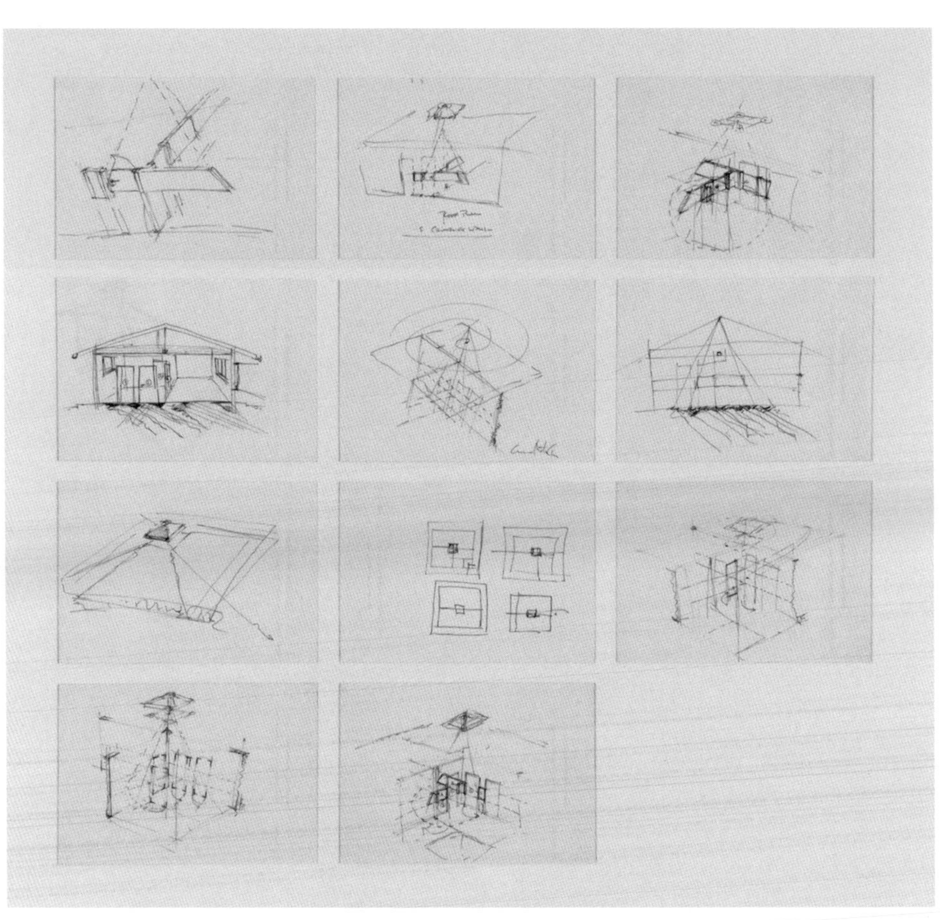

Λ 102
Gordon Matta Clark
A W-Hole House
drawings
Genoa, Galleria Forma, 1973
CCA collection
Montreal

Λ 103
Gordon Matta Clark
A W-Hole House
Roof top atrium cut
Genoa, Galleria Forma, 1973
CCA collection
Montreal

QUESTO eccezionale documento umano trasferisce il lettore al centro dell'officina ideologica di Jean-Paul Sartre, il quale a sessantasette anni resta uno dei personaggi più inquieti dell'intellighenzia europea. L'intervista trabocca di dichiarazioni, confidenze, confessioni di cui lo stesso scrittore tiene a sottolineare la spontaneità imprevedibile e perfino contraddittoria. A differenza di tanti altri intellettuali di alta statura e dotati d'intenzioni profetiche qui Sartre si scopre con una prodigalità quasi temeraria. Si capisce subito che egli è il primo ad appassionarsi come artista al tema autobiografico che anima queste pagine, e a cogliere quel tanto di ambiguità che è connessa alla propria attuale funzione sociale. La storia ch'egli racconta è quella di un intellettuale borghese supernutrito di cultura classica che volontariamente s'è scelto un ruolo di iconoclasta, ma ha la vaga coscienza che fra le icone destinate alla distruzione ce ne sono alcune (forse anche molte) la cui polverizzazione gli darebbe dolore. Ma questo non toglie valore alla sua testimonianza; al contrario ne esalta la drammatica vivacità.

DA *L'ESPRESSO*, 11 FEBBRAIO 1973

Design Leonardo Matt

L. 2.500 (2.358)

anarchitecture 1973

"This term does not imply anti-architecture, but rather is an attempt at clarifying ideas about space which are personal insights and reactions rather than formal socio-political statements."

Letter from
Gordon Matta-Clark to Robert Lendenfrost
World Trade Center, New York,
January 21, 1975

Anarchitecture Group was founded by Gordon Matta-Clark in December 1973.

List of anarchitecture members:

Laurie Anderson	writer, performance, film
Joel Fisher	painter, sculptor, performance
Tina Girouard	dance, stage design, video
Susan Harris	choreography, sculptor, video
Jen Heighstein	sculptor
Bernard Kirschenbaum	engineer, architect, sculptor
Richard Landry	musician, composer, photographer
Max Newhous	electronic music, flutist
Richard Nonas	sculptor
Alan Saret	environmental sculptor, performer

< 104
Gianni Pettena
L'anarchitetto
back cover
1973

Quemlloke il giorno 3.12.75 ← 24/V/73

WORKS BY GORDON MATTA-CLARK
AT GALLERIA FORMA

WORKS BROUGHT FROM NEW YORK.

WALLS PAPER BOOK 4 COPIES ? } $ 10
WALLS PAPER SHEETS (~~2~~ 9) }
~~PHOTOGRAPHS # 7070-8193 50 cm x 100 $ 80~~
RESUMES ~~PHOTOS~~:
1. PIER IN-OUT (2 SHOTS) $ 400
2. 4 WAY WALL (2 SHOTS) $ 400
3 INFRA FORM (5 SHOTS) $ ~~150~~ ~~200~~ 150
4. BRONX FLOOR (5 SHOTS) $ 150
5.) FLOOR ABOVE CEILING BELOW (4 SHOTS) $ 100
6.) THREE HOLE (4 SHOTS) $ 100

WORKS DONE ~~FOR~~ IN GENOA

SCULPTURE:
ROOF-TOP 1M x 1M. $
CENTER-CUT 2.5M x 2M x 58 cm $
PHOTOS:
ATRIUM (3 SETS) (MOUNTED) 78 x 70 $ 260
4 PLY DISPLAY 30 cm x 2M " 550
CORE CUT → 48 cm x 3.40 " 360
A WALL BEFORE 48 cm x 4.50M " 400
DRAWINGS:
INFRA-FORM 1 (CORNERS PROJECT [98 x 69 cm] 350
INFRA-FORM 2 (PERSPECTIVE) [98 x 69 cm] 350
INFRA FORM 3 (CORE) [98 x 69 cm] 350
UNDER CUT 4 [64 x 44] 350
UNDER CUT 5 [[illegible] x 44] $ 250

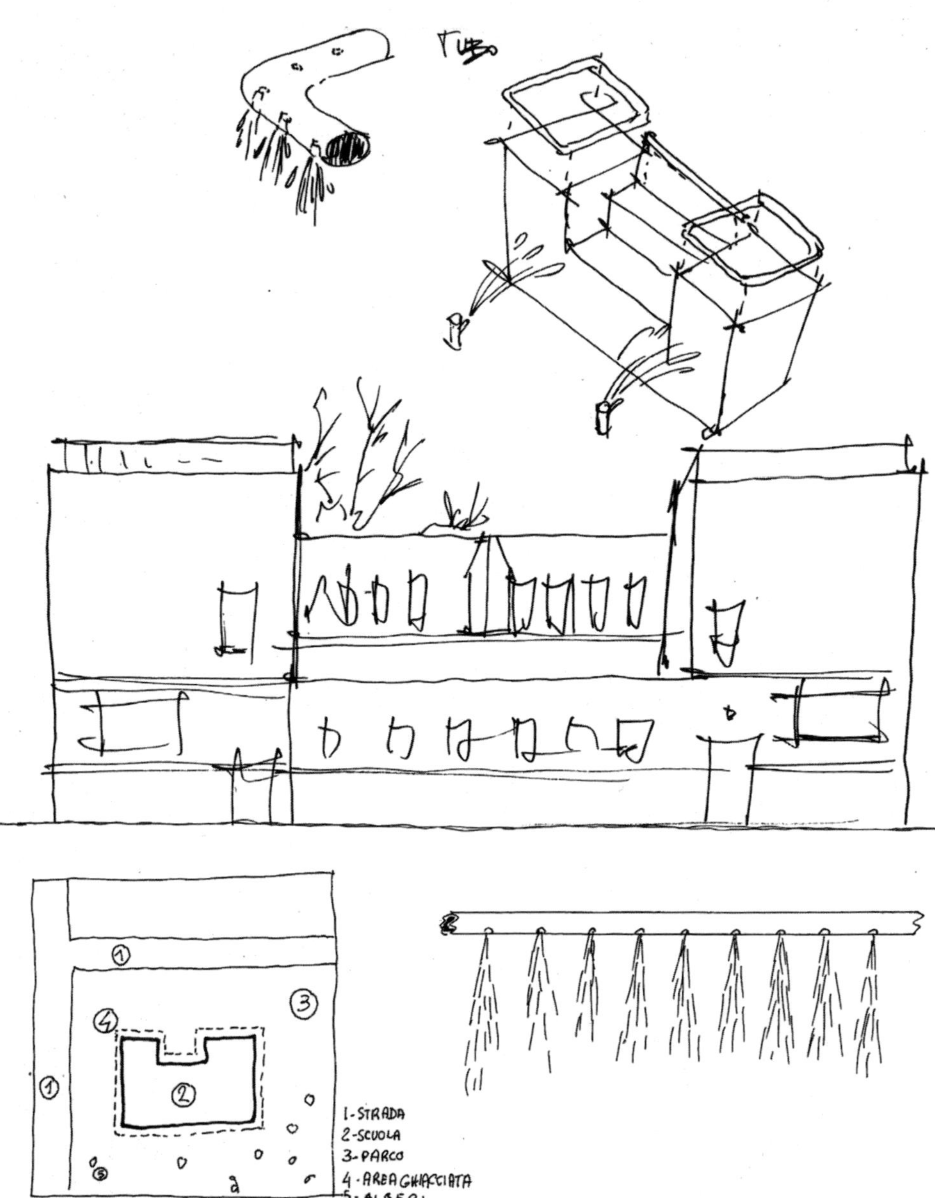

< 106
Gordon Matta Clark
A W-Hole House
agreement
Genoa, Galleria Forma, 1973
Archivio d' Arte
contemporanea, Università
degli Studi di Genova (DIRAAS)

∧ 107
Gianni Pettena
Ice House I
Minneapolis, USA, 1971
Gianni Pettena Archive
Fiesole

Dialogues: Emanuele Piccardo and Gianni Pettena

Interview
Fiesole, Italy
8 Jan. 2014

EP

In your Italian works — the so-called *'trylogy'*, *Carabinieri*, *Milite Ignoto*, *Grazia&Giustizia* — the action takes place in the public space, like an Italian piazza, but when you go to the US your approach changes. Why?

GP

When I went to the States my idea was that of finding a location, a place, where my work could be made without the heavy presence of the past, like in Europe. In fact, in Europe you can't drive or walk, you can't go around without being forced to confront yourself with the traces of the past. Europe is a fabric made up by different layers of previous conceptual, political and theoretical strategies which has formed itself throughout centuries, throughout thousands of years. So, what remains for you to do is acting somehow in a physical context, like a town, working in the holes this fabric has. Where the fabric seems to have a problem, a hole, then your role becomes that of making a mending in the urban fabric, something like that. You always have to draw on a sheet of paper where there are already traces of previous interventions. The meaning of going to the States, and wondering through deserts, was for me like working on a blank sheet of paper, finding at last a context that didn't have any human trace, no previous intervention physically appearing, thus conditioning your freedom. However, dealing with what appeared to be an untouched context like the desert, I discovered that it also contained traces, even if not physical, of previous uses. The deserts of the South West were the living context of the American natives that had, and still have in certain places, a nomadic condition. They recognized architecture in nature, while for us Monument Valley is for instance only the background of John Ford's movies...

EP

Is it true that you translated that experience in your photographic work *About non conscious* architecture?

GP

Yes. Monument Valley is not a valley of monuments.
For the Navajos living there also today it is the valley of their temples. And also the villages and pueblos that you find all around the South West... There are villages inside these enormous caves.

That is, they somehow furnish a cavern that they then adopt as a house during their migrations. When you are in a nomadic condition you are part of nature, you have an osmotic relationship with nature. The moment you build a wall, this is the signal that you abandon your nomadic condition, and you become fixed in a place, so you aren't integrated with nature anymore but nature becomes your counterpart. Through that wall you go, you see and control nature. If nature is properly acting your cultivations are safe, the animals that your raising are safe, etc...

EP

In 1971, in Minneapolis you explored the concept of nature into the city...

GP

Both in Minneapolis and in Salt Lake City. By adopting nature as the director of the game I also tried to make a statement:
that nature and not man is the director of all strategies. Man can only make gestures of violence against nature. Those were the years in which also there were different points of view, in my generation of the sixties-seventies, on this issue...
I emphasize the use of nature. Architecture has to be back to those kinds of attitudes, architecture has to respect nature.

EP

Was the contributions of the students important in the projects that you realized in America?
Can you tell me something about this experience?

GP

I was in Minneapolis invited as an artist in residence at the School of Arts, while in Salt lake City I was a teacher of the fourth year at the Department of Architecture of the University of Utah.
There, in both the two cities, being a young teacher (I was thirty one years old) I was assigning a project to my students and I was working in those project too, and this was not (and is not) usual for a teacher. Generally the teacher gives an assignment to the students and does not confront himself too with that, but just controls what the students do. But also, sometimes, with some students we had a similar age because I also had veterans as students. So, the students were also helping me in making my own installations, in realizing, making my projects visible.

EP

I think that your American work is the real Pettena's work, more than the Italian work of those years that was often influenced by the political context...

GP

Sure, because those works are finally dealing with a context, a term that didn't mean something as complicated as what you could find in Europe. When I was studying architecture — I started at the beginning of the Sixties, I graduated in March 1968 — my artistic activity in Italy (and Europe) was conditioned by the very heavy presence of the past, in any kind of condition. In America I could at last deal with a context much less heavy than in Europe, with much more freedom, till the point that, when I was in Salt Lake City, I also realized that the best way to make architecture is to recognize it in nature. I found out that the architecture of the native Americans was the conceptually highest level you could make architecture, by not making it but discovering it in nature.

EP

In 1972 you met Robert Smithson and you had with him a conversation about his works that was published in the architecture magazine Domus.

GP

Yes, but I had met him before that, in 1969 in Rome when he made *Asphalt Rundown* for the gallery L'Attico directed by Fabio Sargentini, and I found him by chance in Salt Lake City while walking along Main street. He was walking on the same side in the opposite direction. We recognized each other and at the same time we said "What are you doing here?". I invited him to drink a beer in my rented apartment, that was nearby.

EP

This is very funny! But you and Smithson have a different perception of nature and of the relationship between architecture and nature, another kind of approach...

GP

We were both in love with the discovery of the conical copper mine, near Salt Lake City, an incredible open pit. He made a small sketch of that mine, with an intervention by him just at the bottom of it.

This is the difference between him and me, for example.
What I had done instead was to fly over it just to take a picture of the inside of the mine without having to do anything more, because for me that was the most important environment man had built in history, excavating an entire mountain as a reverse cone just for practical reasons. I was able to read in that mine the incredible visual quality of the result of man's work, of that unbelievable environment that was done in that manner not to have any visual or conceptual consequence. This was a monument to work.
About two hundred people had worked with machines for eighty years and that was what could be seen.
For me it was enough just recording it. I didn't need to make a sign to emphasize the fact that I was 'reading' it. Like many other times in the deserts, where I also only took pictures, and I collected and organized them as About non conscious architecture, thus speaking about nature used as architecture by the native Americans.

EP

In 1972 Emilio Ambasz organized *Italy: the new domestic landscape* an exhibition at the MoMA that featured traditional Italian designers, such as Marco Zanuso, Mario Bellini, Gae Aulenti, together with radicals designers such as Archizoom, Superstudio, La Pietra, 9999, Gruppo Strum. The only one among the radical architects to refuse the invitation was Gianni Pettena, and you instead had chosen an exhibition at the famous John Weber Gallery. Why this choice?

GP

Yes, I refused to participate to the exhibition at the MoMA and instead three or four months before I had an exhibition at the John Weber Gallery, in the same building where also the Ileana Sonnabend Gallery, and the Leo Castelli one were located.
At John Weber's I showed my American works, to point out that I was part of a debate about environment and space performed by artists and not by architects. I think that the most important contribution to the architectural debate in the last forty years has been done and performed by artists. There are many architects that have debts towards the work of artists, starting from John Hejduk,Peter Eisenman, till Richard Meier and many others.
Architects that never recognized these debts. I was feeling different from a professional architect. I did not want to use my idea of architecture for a personal profit. I wanted to make architecture

with the tools of arts or the artist, not with the tools of the architect even if I was a licensed architect. I was in the same condition, in those years, as Gordon Matta Clark, that had also had very regular studies and had graduated as an architect. I was somehow more attracted by Robert Smithson because his theories were in some ways more similar to mine. I wanted to emphasize the rule that nature had in our conceptual strategies, and I didn't even want to make violence to architecture like Gordon Matta was making. My approach was a little bit softer. It's true that I was using abandoned buildings, but to cover them with ice, or I was making architecture like the Tumbleweeds Catcher, in Salt Lake City, just for hosting ideas. For hosting your own ideas not functions, even if one morning going there to take pictures when it was still dark I discovered that my work had been totally occupied by birds that apparently were finding that that multistoried-high building was the proper one for them. Also the Clay House was a house inhabited by the family of a colleague of mine at the University, to whom I had asked if it was possible to cover his house with the clay. So we did it, and at the end he recorded everything, not only the Clay House, but then also the Tumbleweeds Catcher and the Red Line, this one even flying over it with his small plane...

EP

All of those works are in the city not in a natural context.

GP

Yes, it is nature that claims its rule in an urban context and also the Red Line, that was a line physically painted of the actual city limit, was meant to emphasize the fact that the city limit is just a line designed on a map and does not work as a real border. It's only a bureaucratic border...

EP

In 1972 you wrote the book *L'anarchitetto* that was published in 1973, the same year in which Gordon Matta-Clark founded the Anarchitecture group. Is there a relationship between these two facts?

GP

No, there is not a relationship. I was making performances and installations of a different kind in those years, and we did not know each other. I wrote *L'anarchitetto* in november-december 1972, the book came out in March 1973 and he founded the group in June. Things went that way around, we didn't have a debate together. We met and we confronted each other... I had a lot of respect for his work but we didn't have a chance to work together.

Λ 115
Gianni Pettena
Red Line performance
Salt Lake City, USA, 1972
Gianni Pettena Archive
Fiesole

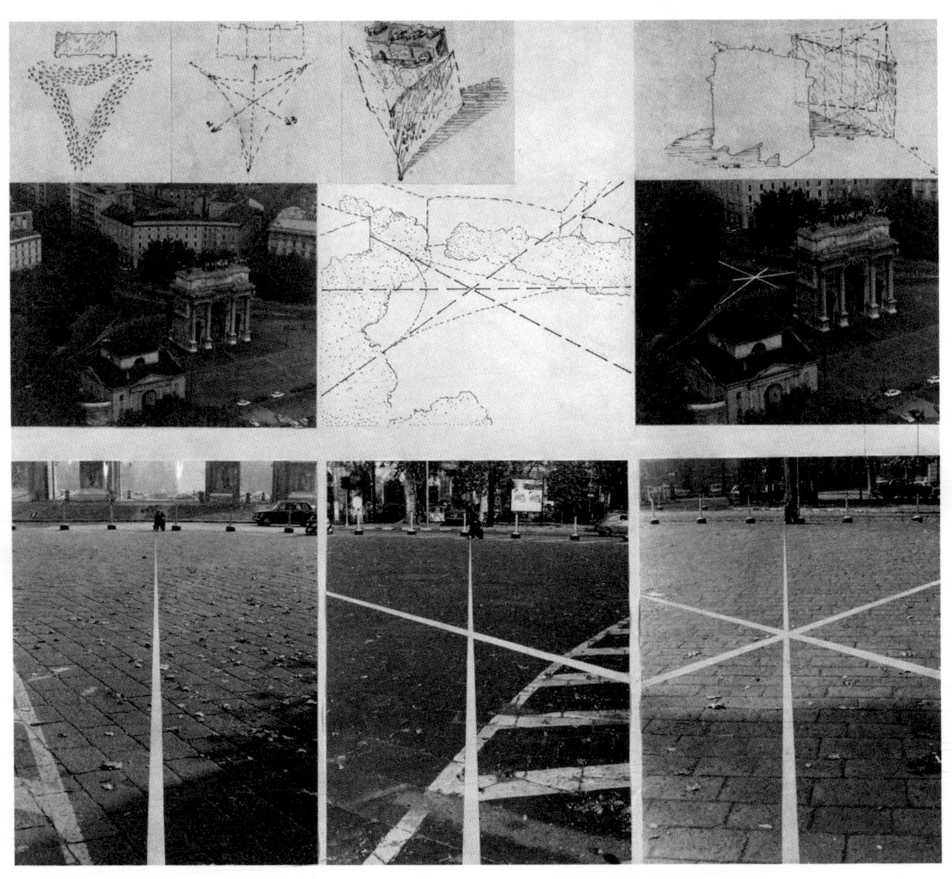

Λ 116
Ugo La Pietra
Sistema disequilibrante
La conquista dello spazio
Milan, 1971
Ugo La Pietra Archive
Milan

Λ 117 > 118 – 119
Gianni Pettena
Red Line performance
Salt Lake City, USA, 1972
Gianni Pettena Archive
Fiesole

KEEP

Dialogues: Emanuele Piccardo and Fabio Sargentini

Interview
Rome, Italy
15 Oct. 2013

EP

Fabio Sargentini, you opened the gallery L`Attico in 1968 and left your father, who owned an art gallery himself...

FS

I left my father's activity in 1966 in order to stay with my generation`s people: Pino Pascali, Jannis Kounellis, Eliseo Mattiacci...These artists were all in their Thirties, and I was only a few years younger. I remember the Pop Art exhibition at the Biennale in Venice in 1964, it created a huge gap with the people of my father`s generation. A true fascination toward Pop Art was born in the Roman artists Mario Schifano and Mario Ceroli. In fact, the Sixties in Rome were amazingly creative years. I opened the gallery on my own, even if I still workeded for a while in my father`s gallery L`Attico in Piazza di Spagna. Our fracture happened because of Pino Pascali, whose work my father did not understand:
while I wanted to work with the artists of my generation, he still wanted to follow his path with the informal painters and the surrealists. With L`Attico I have changed the concept of Art Gallery. In those years, in the United States especially, the art galleries were to be found inside of skyscrapers. You had to take an elevator up to the twelth floor to find them, close to hairdressers' parlours and lawyers' offices. At the end of 1968 I opened the gallery, it was a garage, a real underground space; only afterwords I have notice how ironical it was to have called it L`Attico. It was a space breaking with traditions indeed, and the critics found it difficult to understand it at first, then they got used to it. I wanted the space to remain the same, without any furniture and decoration, void, a memory of what it used to be in the past: a garage. I started with movies' projections at first: a short film by Jean-Luc Godard on the French May and two movies of Alfredo Leonardi, the firts one on the Living Theater, and the second was Libro dei Santi di Roma Eterna, featuring Pino Pascali, Yannis Kounellis, Peter Hartmann, Eliseo Mattiacci, Ettore Rosboch e Mario Schifano. A very important person I met was the Italo-American dancer Simone Forti, born in Florence, she moved to the United States because of the Race Laws. She had studied with Anna Halprin and married Robert Whitman, the most important artist in the Happening scene, even if most people thought that Kaprow was the most influential one, he was primarily a theorist. Forti was also married with Robert Morris before, and when she arrived in Rome in 1968, she had just diverced him. She was the one talking to me about the New York scene, and the performance

world, almost unknown at the time, and of the cooperation between music bands and dancers, like it happened for the project 9 Evenings: Theatre and Engineering — a series of performances organized by some engineers and artists at the Bell Laboratories in New Jersey between the 13th and 23rd of October 1966. Artists such as John Cage, Robert Whitman and Robert Rauschenberg, among the others were part of this work. The performance was an alphabet of the body; there was a complete denial of the literary use of words and text in the concept of it.

EP

L`Attico was an avant-garde exhibition space, a non conventional space also for the American standards...

FS

It is true, a space of that kind was conceived for a form of art that was shaping its self-awareness and the Italians were not enough for a space like that, and therefore I needed the Americans too. They had the right mind frame, I have derived this opinion from Simone Forti. In April 1969 I went to NY with her and met Trisha Brown, Yvonne Rainer, and the gallerist John Weber. It was Weber, married with Annina Nosei from Rome, who agreed with me showing Sol Lewitt at my gallery in may 1969, just before the music and dance festival that we organized with Simone's friends. The people entering the empty garage could not see the graffiti by Lewitt, they were not so evident in fact. I took also an agreement with Weber for the show of Bob Smithson.

EP

Mr Sargentini, you invited Robert Smithon to show his works in 1969...

FS

Smithson wanted to work outside anyway, and used the gallery only for displaying some mud heaps with mirror's spikes embedded inside of them. The outside action was very important to him, and I managed to get the permission to do an action along the *Via Laurentina*: liquid, boiling tar was dripping from a truck down on a slope, leaving a very strong trace on the steep incline. The iconic photography of the action exists only because I personally woke up the photographer Claudio Abate, and we went together at the pawnbroker, that had his camera, and got it back. Smithson went almost crazy, as after two days the pictures and posters were ready.

He knew how to show his friends in the United States the result of his work. In May 1967 I still used L'Attico in Piazza di Spagna to organize the exhibition "Fuoco, Immagine, Acqua, Terra", in spite I had already left my father. It has been the first Arte Povera show, even if this name did not exist yet. I know that Germano Celant does not necessarily agree with me, this one was the first exhibit comprising the artists Pascali, Kounellis, Pistoletto, Ceroli, Gilardi and Schifano. In fact, he also made a show with them, the same year, but only later on in October in Genoa.

EP

Do think that L'Attico in Rome and Galleria Sperone in Turin can be considered the places where artists could experiment more daring and more incisively?

FS

Certainly I do. Milan was not a part of the art scene in those years; it has been only later on with Franco Toselli that the situation improved. It was Gian Enzo Sperone and I that brought our artists to an International standing. When I organized the exhibition of Gino De Dominicis, he was still a new, groundbreaking artist with a certain Duchamp influence, proposing the invisibility of artwork. I have done it Toselli's gallery, and this confirms that we shared the same ideas.

EP

Talking again of Smithson, who were the participants to his action?

FS

We were a small group of friends, Smithsom and his wife Nancy Holt, and the photographer. We choose the area of the Laurentina, as it was rapidly changing, and therefore it was much easier to be proposed as the location for an action like that. Some kind of epic character was driving the truck. In one year or two that area had completely changed. Some people asked me if it was still possible to recognize it, of course it was not. Smithson made some drawings for Asphalt Rundown, and they can be very useful to you, they are still unpublished and the Americans do not know them…

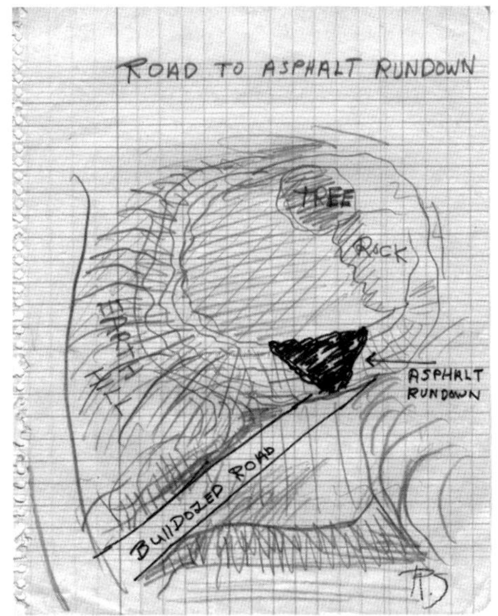

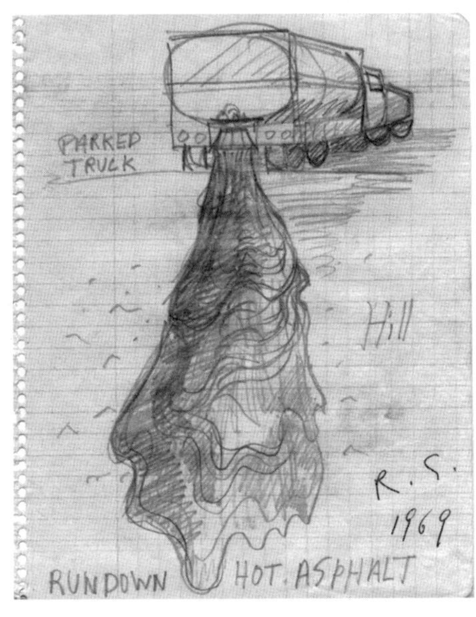

Λ 125 > 126 – 127
Robert Smithson
Asphalt Rundown
sketches and poster
Galleria L'Attico, Rome, 1969
L'Attico-Fabio Sargentini Archive
Rome

Supplies Needed

1. 5 mirrors 4' x 4' x 1/8" thick
2. 9 mirrors 1' x 4' x 1/16"
3. 8 mirrors 10" x 10' x 1/8
4. 2 mirrors 2 1/2' x 2 1/2' 1/8

Mud to mixed in wa...

Mud poured over mirrors, leaving edg...

1

2

3

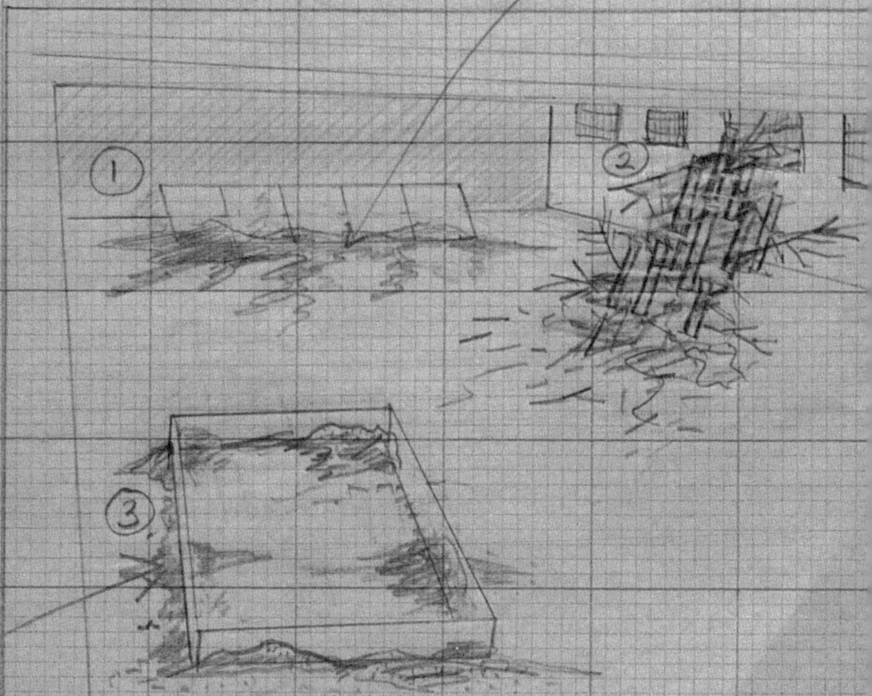

Mirrors shored up by stone + soil perhaps volcanic ash

INSIDE

For Galle... Mirror Proj...

will need shovel

the placement in gallery is subject to change according to material

R. Sm...

<u>OUTSIDE</u> = Materials to be gathered for four sites in Italy. Mirrors to be set up on sites, than mapped + photographed. Would like to visit bubbling mud pools* Mirrors may take different shapes on outdoor sites. Photos of outdoor sites displayed on wall

Mirrors, supported by Roots, vines, sticks ect. (window to be used)

* Near Naples – the <u>Solfatara</u>: mud crust covering sulphur-charged steam – also see Mare Morto + Averno Lake – oyster beds

2½'

2½' mirror

wall

Floor

Split Tree with two 2½' x 2½' mirrors jammed into split. Need steel wedges + sledge hammer and saw

L'Attico Rome ④
for Italy Oct.
69

Superarchitettura Italy 1963-1973:

Gianni Pettena
UFO
Ugo La Pietra
9999
Pietro Derossi
Superstudio

NIER

MILITE IGNOTO

< 130 – 132 ∧ 133 > 134–135
Gianni Pettena
Trilogia: Carabinieri,
Milite Ignoto, Grazia&Giustizia
Installations at Novara,
Ferrara and Palermo, 1968
Gianni Pettena Archive
Fiesole

TAXI

restaurant

Λ 136
UFO
Urboeffimero n.5
Performance
Florence, 1968
UFO Archive
Florence

Λ 137
UFO
Urboeffimero n.6
Performance
Florence, 1968
UFO Archive
Florence

< 138 Λ 139
Ugo La Pietra
Copro una strada e ne faccio un'altra
Campo urbano
Como, 1969
Ugo La Pietra Archive
Milan

> 140 – 141
Gianni Pettena
Dialogo con Arnolfo
Installation
6th Premio Masaccio
San Giovanni Valdarno, 1968
Gianni Pettena Archive
Fiesole

< 142 ∧ 143 > 144 – 145
UFO
Superurbeffimero n.7
6th Premio Masaccio
Performance
San Giovanni Valdarno, 1968
UFO archive
Florence

elemento prefabbricato
per una nuova architettura
toscana
made in ufo

< 146 ∧ 147 > 148 – 149
9999
Happening on Ponte Vecchio
video-projection
Florence, 1968
Carlo Caldini Archive
Florence

Λ 150
Ugo La Pietra
Immersioni nell'acqua
Milan 1970
Ugo La Pietra Archive
Milan

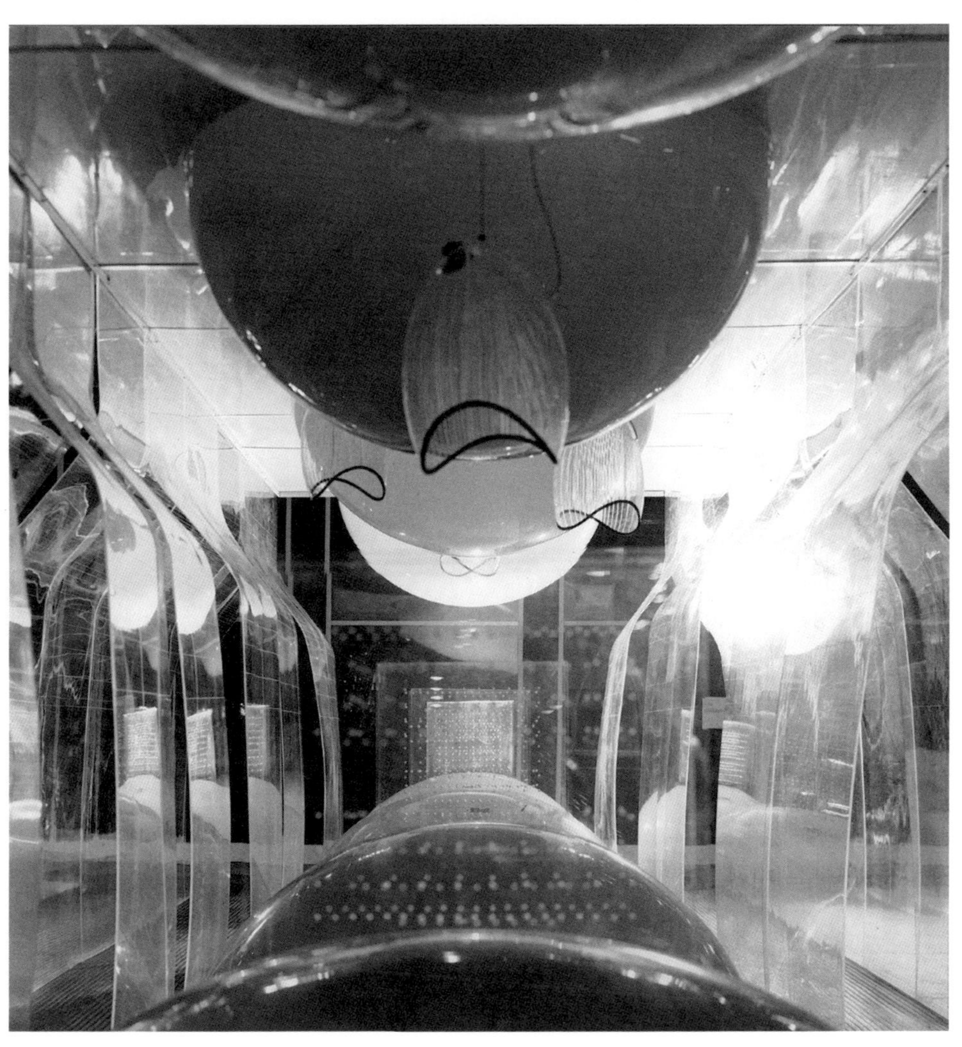

Λ 151
Ugo La Pietra
Immersioni
environment audio-visual
XIV Triennale, Milan, 1968
Ugo La Pietra Archive
Milan

Λ 153
Pietro Derossi
Teatro XIV Triennale
Milan, 1968
Pietro Derossi Archive
Turin

Λ 153
Pietro Derossi
(with Giorgio Ceretti)
E' la fine del mondo
Artists of Arte Povera
Turin, 1966
Pietro Derossi Archive
Turin

> 154 – 155
Pietro Derossi
(with Giorgio Ceretti)
E' la fine del mondo
discotheque
Turin, 1966
Pietro Derossi Archive
Turin

< 156 Λ 157
Superstudio
Mach2
discotheque
Florence, 1967
photographs by
Cristiano Toraldo di Francia
Archive

< 158 Λ 159 > 160 – 161
9999
Space electronic
discotheque *1969*
S-Space festival
Florence, 1971
Carlo Caldini Archive
Florence

< 162 ∧ 163 > 164 – 165
9999
Space electronic
San Francesco
cantico delle creature
and the media
S-Space Mondial Festival,
Florence
1971
Carlo Caldini Archive
Florence

< 166 – 168 ∧ 169
UFO
Bamba Issa 1
discotheque
Forte dei Marmi, 1969
UFO Archive
Florence

ATTENZI
PERICO

Emanuele Piccardo

Piccardo, is an architect, photographer, filmmaker, and curator. In 2002, he founded the architecture magazine Archphoto.it. In 2011 he founded the magazine archphoto 2.0, the printed upgrated version of Archphoto.it, part of the project Archizines curated by Elias Redstone. Since 2005 Piccardo has curated architectural research about the Superarchitettura, most recently the exhibition Radical City in Turin (2012). As a photographer and filmmaker he has exhibited in the Bibliothèque Nationale de France, Paris; the MAXXI Museum, Rome; and the Milan Triennale. His documentary films include Fango about the flooding in Italy (2012; Award of Excellence, Los Angeles Movie Award) and Lettera22 (2009, Award of Best Architecture Film, International Asolo Art Film Festival, Official selection Architecture Film Festival Rotterdam) about the entrepreneur Adriano Olivetti. His lecture were made at Princeton University, Pratt Institute, IUAV, Politecnico di Milano. In 2013 He won the Graham Foundation Award.

Amit Wolf

Wolf is an architect, a writer and a curator. His atelier is dedicated to developing varied commercial and residential projects in the Los Angeles area. He has curated several exhibitions and events collaboratively in Los Angeles. He is currently working on the *Casa dei Robot* pavilion at the 2014 Venice Biennale. Wolf teaches courses in architecture history and theory at SCI-Arc. He previously taught at Otis, Woodbury University, and UCLA. Wolf is the recipient of the 2007 Clinton Webb Award, the 2012 California Interdisciplinary Consortium of Italian Studies Award, and the 2013 Graham Foundation Award. Wolf's publications have to date focused on the areas of Italian experimentalist practice as well as on theoretical issues in contemporary architecture. His *Fabrication and Fabrication* (2014) explores computational advances in the field. Wolf received his Master of Architecture degree from the Politecnico di Milano in 2001. He received his Doctor of Philosophy in the History, Theory and Criticism of Architecture and Art from UCLA in 2012.

Beyond
Environment

The publication was made possible
by generous grants of the
Graham Foundation and of the
Woodbury University

Published by:
Actar Publishers
151 Grand ST, 5th Fl.,
New York, NY 10013, USA

Cover photo:
© Gianni Pettena, *Ice house II*

Editors and concept:
Emanuele Piccardo, Amit Wolf

Copy Editors:
Kevin McMahon, David Heymann,
Julian Ma, Jordan Squires

Translators from Italian:
Alessandra Natale, Amit Wolf

Graphic:
Artiva Design

Printing and binding:
Grafos S.A.

Cataloging-in-Publication data
for this book is available from the
Library of Congress.

First edition – 2014
Printed and bound in the European Union

Emanuele Piccardo and Amit Wolf
would like to greatly thank:
Claudio Abate, Claudia Baghino,
Herwig Baumgartner, Tamara Bloomberg,
Lapo Binazzi, Carlo Caldini, Toni Carta,
Andrea Dapueto, Pietro Derossi,
Piero Frassinelli, Todd Gannon,
David Heymann, Caterina Iaquinta,
Ugo La Pietra, Kevin Mcmahon,
Paolo Minetti, Alessandra Natale,
Bruno Orlandoni, Marco Pace,
Gianni Pettena, Stefania Coppi Pettena,
Marzia Ratti, Ingalill Wahlroos-Ritter,
Fabio Sargentini, Cristiano Toraldo di Francia.

Special thanks goes to these institutions:
The Graham Foundation
Woodbury School of Architecture, Burbank
WUHO Gallery, Los Angeles
LACE Gallery, Los Angeles
The Getty Research Institute, Los Angeles
Artist Right Society, New York
Allan Kaprow Estate, Encinitas
Canadian Centre for Architecture, Montréal

Distribution:

Actar D, Inc.
151 Grand ST, 5th Fl.,
New York, NY 10013, USA
www.actar-d.com

North America & Asia
Actar D Inc.
orders@actar-d.com

Europe, Middle East & Japan
Marston Book Services Ltd,
160 Milton Park, Abingdon
OX14 4SD, UK
trade.orders@marston.co.uk

ISBN 978-1-940291-33-8